PIONEERS OF THE PACIFIC COAST

PIONEERS OF THE PACIFIC COAST

A CHRONICLE OF SEA ROVERS AND FUR HUNTERS

AGNES C. LAUT

Introduction by
ROSEMARY NEERING

TouchWood
Editions

TouchWood Editions
www.touchwoodeditions.com

LIBRARY AND ARCHIVES CANADA CATALOGUING IN PUBLICATION
Laut, Agnes C. (Agnes Christina), 1871–1936
Pioneers of the Pacific coast: a chronicle of sea rovers and fur hunters
/ by Agnes C. Laut.

Includes index.
Originally published: Toronto: Glasgow, Brook & Co., 1915.

Print format: ISBN 978-1-926971-00-1
Electronic monograph in PDF format: ISBN 978-1-926971-01-8
Electronic monograph in HTML format: ISBN 978-1-926971-02-5

1. Northwest Coast of North America—Discovery and exploration.
2. Pacific Coast (North America)—Discovery and exploration.
3. British Columbia—Discovery and exploration. I. Title.

FC3821.2.L38 2011   910.9164'3   C2010-907499-8

Proofreader: Holland Gidney
Cover image: *The Descent Of The Fraser River, 1808*
From a colour drawing by C.W. Jefferys

We gratefully acknowledge the financial support for our publishing activities
from the Government of Canada through the Canada Book Fund, Canada
Council for the Arts, and the province of British Columbia through the
British Columbia Arts Council and the Book Publishing Tax Credit.

The interior pages of this book have been printed on 100% post-consumer
recycled paper, processed chlorine free, and printed with vegetable-based inks.

1 2 3 4 5 14 13 12 11

PRINTED IN CANADA

The Descent of the Fraser River, 1808.
FROM A COLOUR DRAWING BY C.W. JEFFERYS

CONTENTS

❈   ❈   ❈

ILLUSTRATIONS

❈ ❈ ❈

INTRODUCTION
by Rosemary Neering

The first decade of the twentieth century was one of great change for Canada. The country's population grew by more than one-third as immigrants streamed into the west. Alberta and Saskatchewan became new provinces, carved out of the old Northwest Territories. Almost as many people now lived in Canada's cities as lived in small towns and in rural areas. Despite occasional setbacks, the economy was booming. As the country established more distance from Britain, it officially sent troops overseas for the first time, during the Boer War. Events and trends suggested that Sir Wilfrid Laurier had spoken the truth when he suggested in 1904, "I think we can claim that Canada will fill the twentieth century."

Against this backdrop, Canadian publisher Robert Glasgow decided that Canadians needed to know more about this country's history. His first and massive effort was a weighty, twenty-three volume series intended to promote "a broad national spirit in all parts of the Dominion" as the road to "an enlightened patriotism which vibrates to the sentiment of nationality."

That task completed, Glasgow decided to publish a shorter, more accessible version, where the adventures of native peoples, early explorers, colonizers, pioneers, and settlers would be told in simpler language. Such a series could be used in schools, but it would also inform the general public of Canada's heroic past. Thus was born the thirty-two-volume *Chronicles of Canada*.

The books, the size of a modern paperback, one hundred and forty pages long, hardbound in red, with the cover lettered in gold, were published between 1914 and 1916, as Canada helped fight the First World War. Glasgow hired seasoned academics and historians George M. Wrong and H.H. Langton to edit the books. Some of the writers he hired were also academics. William Wood, for example, who wrote a series high of six books, was a historian and long-time fellow of the Royal Society of Canada.

For others, Glasgow chose writers who could produce "freshly written narratives for popular reading." Who better than freelance writers and journalists with a sound grounding in history, and who already knew how to write for the masses? Stephen Leacock, best known for his works of humour, wrote three of the books. For another three, including this volume, Glasgow selected Agnes Laut, a freelance writer of novels, non-fiction books, and articles. Only one other woman was a series author, and she wrote just one book.

He chose well. Born in 1871 in Ontario's Huron County, Laut was just two years old when her family moved to Manitoba. She later recalled that she felt lucky to have been able to spend her early childhood riding "real horses, not rocking horses; sailing real rafts on real creeks, not just blowing paper boats on a bathtub; hunting the secret nooks of live, real woodland things . . ."[1]

She was doubly lucky to have arrived in the West at a tumultuous time. The first Riel Rebellion, pitting the Métis of Red River against incoming settlers, took place in 1870. The second, when the native peoples of the northwest joined with the Métis, to seek better treatment from the Canadian government, occurred in 1885—as did Louis Riel's execution. The first train from the United States drew into Winnipeg in 1878; the trans-Canada railway was completed in 1885, when Laut was just fourteen. Before she turned sixteen, she saw the first wheat exported from Manitoba, the first telephone installed in Winnipeg, and the first horse-drawn streetcars trundling along the city's streets. Yet life in her West encompassed more than technological change. Fur traders still brought pelts from the plains to Winnipeg markets, native peoples still ranged the prairie and the hills, the buffalo had not yet all been exterminated, and the old native, Métis, explorer and adventurer stories were frequently retold.

This rich and vivid tapestry entranced Laut. A bout of tuberculosis forced her from her university studies when she was twenty, and she retreated to a wilderness ranch to recuperate. She said the experience changed her life. From that time on, she travelled exhaustively throughout the West, and was soon earning her living from writing about the land and people she loved.

For two years, from age twenty-four to twenty-six, she worked as an editorial writer for the *Manitoba Free Press*. She then turned to freelancing and spent the rest of her life in that career. She moved to the United States at some point, to be closer to her markets; but she was not homebound. According to biographer Valerie Legge, Laut spent three months of every year living as a tramp and a woodsman, camping, she claimed, in every Canadian and American national park but two. In 1929, now fifty-eight years old, she wrote to a correspondent that she had been "going West for the past six years by way of Seattle . . . just back from Wyoming now."[2]

Laut's travels and research, backed by her fascination with the place and time, provided the base for her swashbuckling novels of the Canadian and America West. They explore, with drama and vividness, the lives of the men and women who wandered and lived in the region.

Her non-fiction was somewhat more straightforward. She sold articles to publications such as *Harper's*, the *Saturday Evening Post*, *Collier's*, the *American Review of Books*, *Century Magazine*, and *Outings*, on a variety of topics from travel to the fur trade to farming to "Oriental" immigration to Russian sealers on the Pacific coast. In 1912, she was commissioned by *Saturday Night* magazine to report on Asian immigration and the Wobblies union movement in British Columbia. Her articles on the topics were turned into a pamphlet and widely sold.

Laut's growing reputation and her interest in northwest history convinced publisher Glasgow to hire her to write three books. She did so quickly and professionally. *The 'Adventurers of England' on Hudson's Bay* appeared in 1914, *Pioneers of the Pacific Coast* in 1915, and *The Cariboo Trail* in 1916. While she was working on these books, she also completed *The Canadian Commonwealth*, a somewhat chauvinistic three hundred-and-fifty-page examination of Canada's history and place in the world. Also published in 1914 was a novel she had written in 1909–1910, *Freebooters of the Wilderness*, a book that took on sheep killers, land thieves, and government mismanagement in the American West.

All of her books were marked by a dramatic, sometimes flamboyant, use of language. "Canada has always been free," she exclaimed in her introduction to *The Canadian Commonwealth*, "free as the birds of passage that winged above the canoe of the first voyageur who pointed his craft up the St. Lawrence for the Pacific; but what you do find from the very first is a fight for national existence; and when the fight was won, Canada arose like a wrestler with consciousness of strength for new destiny."[3] Today, we might see some of her writing as overblown, and approaching purple prose. But Laut thought her subjects were wondrous and exciting, and, a story teller at heart, she wanted her readers to experience that wonder and excitement.

The topics, book length, and projected audience for the *Chronicles* series were a fine fit for her approach and writing style. This book, *Pioneers of the Pacific Coast*, number twenty-two in the series, was especially so, since it tells the tales of the adventurers and explorers who made their way by sea and by land along the north Pacific coast of North America. Piratical Francis Drake, ill-fated Vitus Bering, adventuresome James Cook, stoic George Vancouver–even Laut can't make him too exciting–heroic Alexander Mackenzie and Simon Fraser, dogged David Thompson, all take their turn on Laut's stage.

Each man and his deeds intrigued her, and she wanted the reader to experience what these men had experienced—if only to some small degree. Imagine, she exhorts you, men crowded in tiny ships far from home, at the mercy of winds and waves; men tattered and ill and half-starved, pressing on into unmapped and dangerous territory; men lured by the promise of both riches and freedom to an unknown land with unknown hazards and hoped-for rewards. How could one not be captivated by such tales of great adventure? Only if the writing was mundane, a collection of facts, dates, and names, and such writing was not for Laut. She wanted to convey the fear and exultation of every expedition that she chronicled.

Here comes Francis Drake, waving his plumed hat and dealing out wine to his merry boys before he plunders the Spanish fleet. "Yards, sails, masts fell shattered and torn from the Spanish ship. The English clapped their grappling-hooks to her sides, and naked swords did the rest," writes Laut. The poor Mexicans who sailed in Spanish vessels along the coast, "had nothing behind them but the branding iron, or slavery in the mines, if they failed. Yet they sang as they sailed in their rickety ships."

Mackenzie "leaped to the dangerous slope, cut foothold and handhold on the face of the cliff with an axe, and scrambled up to a table of level rock" and is many times a hero in his trek. Fraser faces much adversity with steadfastness and equanimity: "Imagine, for a moment, the scene! The turbid mad waters of the Fraser hemmed in between rock walls, carving a living way through the adamant; banks from which red savages threw down rocks wherever the wild current drove the dug-out ashore; and, tossed by the waves–a chip-like craft containing nineteen ragged men singing like schoolboys!" (Laut, as befit her times, maintained a colonial attitude towards the native peoples, though she often described individual natives in positive ways.)

Thompson finds "crouched between the heavy, dank forests and the heaving river floods . . . a little palisaded and fresh-hewn log fur post," the evidence that he has arrived just too late to claim the mouth of the Columbia River for the British. Laut travels with each man and each expedition, choosing and embellishing the most vivid details, sometimes at the expense of historical fact.

Her *Chronicles* books completed, she continued freelancing and writing books. Though the years from 1900 to 1915 were her most prolific, she wrote several more books on Canada and the United States and many more magazine articles.

She was a fervent collector of western Americana and Canadiana and tells a correspondent that she had to "sell out a lot . . . [of it] before the War or enlarge my house . . . I'm again full up with American and we shall have to tear out an old chimney to make room or sell a few more to make space . . . If I were West, I'd be haunting auction rooms for old books on the early West, keen as a wolf's teeth."[4]

Her own work was harder to come by. She wrote that she did not even have a copy of the first edition of one of her own books. And in another letter, she regrets that she cannot send along a copy of *The Cariboo Road*, for "it went out of print after Mr. Glasgow, the publisher, died and I have never seen even one copy in Rare Book Catalogue."[5]

When she was not travelling, she worked from Wassaic, a small town in New York State, where she lived for many years. "The influx of city people," she wrote, "have changed our simple life but not the repose or beauty of gorgeous gardens."[6] She died in Wassaic in 1936.

[1] As quoted in the introduction to Valerie Legge's *The Lords of the North*, Toronto: Tecumseh Press, 2001, n.p.

[2] Agnes Laut to Mrs. M.E. McVicker, July 15, 1929, held by Special Collections, University of Victoria.

[3] *The Canadian Commonwealth*, Indianapolis: The Bobbs-Merrill Company, 1915, n.p.

[4] Laut to McVicker.

[5] Laut to McVicker, February 4, 1933, held by Special Collections, University of Victoria.

[6] Laut to McVicker, July 15, 1929.

ROSEMARY NEERING has been writing about British Columbia for more than thirty years, always seeking out the unusual and quirky tales that abound in this province's history. The author of *Wild West Women: Travellers, Adventurers and Rebels*, *Down the Road: Journeys Through Small-Town British Columbia* and *A Traveller's Guide to Historic British Columbia*, as well as a number of other works on BC and Canadian history, she has written prolifically for publications such as *British Columbia Magazine*. When she isn't skulking down archival alleyways, you can find Rosemary in Victoria, where she lives with her partner, Joe Thompson, and her cat. She gardens, creates hand-built pottery, and plays tennis and pickleball.

THE VOYAGE OF THE *GOLDEN HIND*

All through the sixteenth century the South Seas were regarded as a mysterious wonder-world, whence Spain drew unlimited wealth of gold and silver bullion, of pearls and precious stones. Spain had declared the Pacific 'a closed sea' to the rest of the world. But in 1567 it happened that Sir John Hawkins, an English mariner, was cruising in the Gulf of Mexico, when a terrific squall, as he said, drove his ships landward to Vera Cruz, and he sent a messenger to the Spanish viceroy there asking permission to dock and repair his battered vessels. Now on one of the English ships was a young officer, not yet twenty-five years of age, named Francis Drake. Twelve Spanish merchantmen rigged as frigates lay in the harbour, and Drake observed that cargo of small bulk but ponderous weight, and evidently precious, was being stowed in their capacious holds. Was this the gold and silver bullion that was enriching Spain beyond men's dreams? Whence did it come? Could English privateers intercept it on the high seas?

Perhaps the English adventurers evinced too great interest in that precious cargo; for though the Spanish governor had granted them permission to repair their ships, the English had barely dismantled when Spanish fire-ships came drifting down on their moorings. A cannon-shot knocked a mug of beer from Hawkins's hand, and head over heels he fell into the sea, while a thousand Spaniards began sabring the English crew ashore. Some friendly hand threw out a rope to Hawkins, who was clad in complete armour. In the dark, unseen by the enemy, he pulled himself up the side of a smaller ship, and, cutting hawsers, scudded for the open sea. There escaped, also, of Hawkins's fleet another small ship, which was commanded by Francis Drake; and after much suffering both vessels reached England.

One can imagine the effect on young Drake of the treacherous act and of the glimpse of that cargo of gold and silver treasure. The English captains had but asked a night's lodging from a power supposed to be friendly. They had been met by a pirate raid. Good! Young Francis Drake eagerly took up Spain's challenge; he would meet the raid with counter-raid. Three years later he was cruising the Spanish Main, capturing and plundering ships and forts and towns. In 1572 he led his men across the Isthmus of Panama, and intercepted and captured a Spanish convoy of treasure coming overland. Near the south side of the isthmus he climbed a tree and had his first glimpse of the Pacific. It set his blood on the leap. On bended knee he prayed aloud to the Almighty to be permitted to sail the first English ship on that 'faire sea.' And, having recrossed the isthmus and loaded his ships with plunder, he bore away for England and reached Plymouth in August 1573.

The raid on Panama had brought Drake enormous wealth. At his own cost he built three frigates and two sloops to explore the South Seas, his purpose being to enter the Pacific through the Strait of Magellan, which no Englishman had yet ventured to pass. These ships he equipped as if for royal tournament. Players of the violin and the harp discoursed music at each meal. Rarest wines filled the lockers. Drake, clad in rich velvet, dined on plates of pure gold served by ten young noblemen, who never sat or donned hat in his presence; and on his own ship, the *Pelican*—afterwards called the *Golden Hind*—he had a hundred picked marines, men eager for battle and skilful in wielding the cutlass. His men loved him as a dauntless leader; they feared him, too, with a fear that commanded obedience on the instant.

Queen Elizabeth was in a quandary how to treat her gallant buccaneer and rover of the high seas. England and Spain were at peace, and she could not give Drake an open royal commission to raid the commerce of a friendly power; but she did present him with a magnificent sword, to signify that she would have no objection if he should cut his way through the portals leading to the 'closed sea.' The fleet set sail in December 1577, and steered by the west coast of Morocco and the Cape Verde Islands. The coast of Brazil was reached in April. Two of the ships were abandoned near the mouth of the Rio de la Plata, after having been stripped of provisions. In August the remaining three ships entered the tempestuous seas around Cape Horn. Drake drove before the gales with sails close-reefed and hatches battened, and came out with only one of his three ships left, the first English keel to cleave the waters of the Pacific. In honour of the feat Drake renamed his ship the *Golden Hind*. Perhaps there was jocose irony in the suggestion of gold and speed. Certain it is, the crew of the *Golden Hind* were well content with the possession of both gold and speed before advancing far up the west coast of South America.

Quite by chance, which seems always to favour the daring, somewhere off the coast of Chile Drake picked up an Indian fisherman. The natives of South America, for the best of reasons, hated their Spanish masters, who enslaved them, treated them brutally, and forced them to work in the pearl fisheries and the mines. Drake persuaded the Indian to pilot his ship into the harbour of Valparaiso. Never dreaming that any foreign vessel had entered the Pacific, Spanish treasure-ships lay rocking to the tide in fancied security, and actually dipped colours to Drake. Drake laughed, waved his plumed hat back in salute, dealt out wine to give courage to 'his merrie boys,' and sailed straight amid the anchored treasure-ships. Barely had the *Golden Hind* taken a position in the midst of the enemy's fleet, when, selecting one of the staunchest vessels of the enemy, Drake had grappling-irons thrown out, clamping his ship to her victim. In a trice the English sailors were on the Spanish deck with swords out and the rallying-cry of 'God and St. George! Down with Spanish dogs!' Dumbfounded and unarmed, down the hatches, over the bulwarks into the sea, reeled the surprised Spaniards. Drake clapped hatches down upon those trapped inside, and turned his cannon on the rest of the unguarded Spanish fleet. Literally, not a drop of blood was shed. The treasure-ships were looted of their cargoes and sent drifting out to sea.

All the other harbours of the Pacific were raided and looted in similar summary fashion; and, somewhere seaward from Lima, Drake learned of a treasure-ship bearing untold riches—the *Glory of the South Seas*—the huge caravel in which the Spaniards sent home to Spain the yearly tribute of bullion. The *Golden Hind*, with her sails spread to the wind, sought for the *Glory* like a harrier for its quarry. One crew of Spaniards on a small ship that was scuttled saved their throats by telling Drake that the great ship was only two days ahead, and loaded to the water-line with wealth untold. Drake crowded sail, had muskets and swords furbished and thirty cannon loaded, and called on his crew to quit themselves like men. And when the wind went down he ordered small boats out to tow the *Golden Hind*. For five days the hunt lasted, never slackening by day or by night; and when, at three in the afternoon of a day in March, Drake's brother shouted from the cross-trees, "Sail ho!" every man aboard went mad with impatience to crowd on the last inch of canvas and overtake the rich prize. The Englishmen saw that the Spanish ship was so heavily laden that she was making but slow progress; and so unconscious was the Spanish captain of danger, that when he discerned a ship approaching he actually lowered canvas and awaited what he thought might be fresh orders from the viceroy. The *Golden Hind* sped on till she was almost alongside the Spaniard; then Drake let go full blast all thirty cannon, as fast as he could shift and veer for the cannoneers to take aim. Yards, sails, masts fell shattered and torn from the splendid Spanish ship. The English clapped their grappling-hooks to her sides, and naked swords did the rest. To save their lives, the Spanish crew, after a feeble resistance, surrendered, and bullion to the value in modern money of almost a million dollars fell into the hands of the men of the *Golden Hind.*

Drake's vessel was now loaded deep with treasure, and preparations were made to sail homeward, but her commander realized that it would be dangerous to attempt to return to England by way of the Spanish Main with a ship so heavily laden that she must sail slowly. It was then that legends of a North-East Passage came into his mind. He would sail northward in search of the strait that was supposed to lead through the continent to the Atlantic—the mythical strait of Anian. As the world knows, there was no such passage; but how far north did Drake sail seeking it? Some accounts say as far as Oregon; others, as far as the northern coast of California; but, at all events, as he advanced farther north he found that the coast sheered farther and farther west. So he gave over his attempt to find the strait of the legends, and turned back and anchored in 'a faire and good bay,' which is now known as Drake's Bay, a short distance north of San Francisco; and, naming the region New Albion, he claimed it for Queen Elizabeth. In July 1579 he weighed anchor and steered south-west. He reached the Molucca Islands in November, and arrived at Java in March. In June he rounded the Cape of Good Hope and then beat his way up the Atlantic to England. In September 1580 the *Golden Hind* entered the harbour of Plymouth. How Drake became the lion of the hour when he reached England, after having circumnavigated the globe, need not be told. Ballads were recited in his honour. Queen Elizabeth dined in state on the *Golden Hind*, and, after the dinner, with the sword which she had given him when he set out, she conferred on Drake the honour of knighthood, as the seal of his country's acclaim.

Drake's conclusions regarding the supposed passage from the Pacific to the Atlantic were correct, though for two hundred years they were rejected by geographers. His words are worth setting down: *'The Asian and American continents, if they be not fully joined, yet seem they to come very neere, from whose high and snow-covered mountains, the north and north-west winds send abroad their frozen nimphes to the infecting of the whole air—hence comes it that in the middest of their summer, the snow hardly departeth from, these hills at all; hence come those thicke mists and lo most stinking fogges, . . . for these reasons we coniecture that either there is no passage at all through these Northerne coasts, which is most likely, or if there be, that it is unnavigable.'*

VITUS BERING ON THE PACIFIC

Since Drake's day more than a century had rolled on. Russia was awakening from ages of sleep, as Japan has awakened in our time, and Peter the Great was endeavouring to pilot the ship of state out to the wide seas of a world destiny. Peter, like the German Kaiser of to-day, was ambitious to make his country a world-power. He had seen enough of Europe to learn that neighbouring nations were increasing their strength in three ways—by conquest, by discovery, and by foreign commerce—and that foreign commerce meant, not only buying and selling, but carrying the traffic of other nations. The East India Company, in whose dockyards he had worked as a carpenter, was a striking instance of the strength that could be built up by foreign commerce. Its ships cruised from Nova Zembla to Persia and East India, carrying forth the products of English workshops and farms, and bringing back the treasures of all lands.

By conquest, Peter had extended the bounds of his empire from the Ural Mountains to the seas of China. By discovery, what remained to be done? France and England had acquired most of the North American continent. Spain and Portugal claimed South America; and Spain had actually warned the rest of the world that the Pacific was 'a closed sea.' But there were legends of a vast domain yet undiscovered. Juan de Fuca, a Greek pilot, employed, as alleged, by Spanish explorers between 1587 and 1592, was reported to have told of a passage from the Pacific to the Arctic through a mountainous forested land up in the region of what is now British Columbia. Whether Juan lied, or mistook his own fancies for facts, or whether the whole story was invented by his chronicler Michael Lok, does not much matter. The fact was that Spanish charts showed extensive unexplored land north of Drake's New Albion or California. At this time geographers had placed on their maps a vast continent called Gamaland between America and Asia; and, as if in corroboration of this fiction, when Peter's Cossacks struggled doggedly across Asia, through Siberia, to the Pacific, people on these far shores told tales of drift-wood coming from America, of islands leading like steps through the sea to America, of a nation like themselves, whose walrus-hide boats sometimes drifted to Siberia and Kamchatka. If any new and wealthy region of the world remained to be discovered, Peter felt that it must be in the North Pacific. When it is recalled that Spain was supposed to have found in Peru temples lined with gold, floors paved with silver, and pearls readily exchanged in bucketfuls for glass beads, it can be realized that the motive for discovery was not merely scientific. It was one that actuated princes and merchants alike. And Peter the Great had an additional motive—the development of his country's merchant shipping. It was this that had induced him to establish the capital of his kingdom on the Baltic. So, in 1725, five weeks before his death—one of the most terrible deaths in history, when remorse and ghosts of terrible memories came to plague his dying hours till his screams could be heard through the palace halls—he issued a commission for one of the greatest expeditions of discovery that ever set out for America—a commission to Vitus Bering, the Dane, to explore the Pacific for Russia.

Like Peter the Great, Vitus Bering had served an apprenticeship with the East India Company. It is more than probable that he first met his royal patron while he was in this service. While other expeditions to explore America had but to cross the sea before beginning their quest, Bering's expedition had to cross the width of Europe, and then the width of Asia, before it could reach even the sea. Between St. Petersburg and the Pacific lay six thousand miles of mountain and tundra. Caravans, flat-boats, and dog-trains must be provided to transport supplies; and the vessels to be used at the end of the land journey must be built on the Pacific. The explorers were commissioned to levy tribute for food and fur on Tartar tribes as their caravans worked slowly eastward. Bering's first voyage does not concern America. He set out from Kamchatka on July 9, 1728, with forty-four men, and sailed far enough north to prove that Asia and America were not united by any Gamaland, and that the strait now bearing his name separated the two continents; but, like the tribes of Siberia, he saw signs of a great land area on the other side of the rain-hidden sea. Out of the blanketing fog drifted trees, seaweed, bits of broken boats. And though Bering, like the English navigator Drake, was convinced that no Gamaland existed, he was confronted by the learned geographers, who had a Gamaland on their maps and demanded truculently, whence came the signs of land?

In March 1730, within one month of the time he returned to St. Petersburg, Bering was again ordered to prepare to carry out the dead emperor's command—'to find and set down reliably what was in the Pacific.' The explorer had now to take his orders from the authorities of the Academy of Sciences, whose bookish inexperience and visionary theories were to hamper him at every turn. Botanists, artists, seven monks, twelve physicians, Cossack soldiers—in all, nearly six hundred men—were to accompany him; and to transport this small army of explorers, four thousand pack-horses were sent winding across the desert wastes of Siberia, with one thousand exiles as guides and boatmen to work the boats and rafts on the rivers and streams. Great blaring of trumpets marked the arrival and departure of the caravans at the Russian forts on the way; and if the savants, whose presence pestered the soul of poor Bering, had been half as keen in overcoming the difficulties of the daily trail as they were in drinking pottle-deep to future successes, there would have been less bickering and delay in reaching the Pacific. Dead horses marked the trail across two continents. The Cossack soldiers deserted and joined the banditti that scoured the Tartar plains; and for three winters the travellers were storm-bound in the mountains of Siberia. But at length they reached Avacha Bay on the eastern shore of Kamchatka, and the waters of the Pacific gladdened the eyes of the weary travellers. At Petropavlovsk on the bay they built a fort, houses, barracks, a chapel, and two vessels, named the *St. Peter* and the *St. Paul*.

Early on the morning of June 4, 1741, the chapel bells were set ringing. At dawn prayers were chanted to invoke the blessing of Heaven on the success of the voyage. Monks in solemn procession paraded to the water's edge, singing. The big, bearded men, who had doggedly, drunkenly, profanely, religiously, marched across deserts and mountains to reach the sea, gave comrades a last fond embrace, ran down the sand, jumped into the jolly-boats, rowed out, and clambered up the ships' ladders. And when the reverberating roll of the fort cannon signalled the hour of departure, anchors were weighed, and sails, loosened from the creaking yard-arms, fluttered and filled to the wind. While the landsmen were still cheering and waving a farewell, Bering and his followers watched the shores slip away, the waters widen, the mountains swim past and back. Then the *St. Peter* and the *St. Paul* headed out proudly to the lazy roll of the ocean.

Now the savants, of whom Bering carried too many with him for his own peace of mind, had averred that he had found no Gamaland on his first voyage because he had sailed too far north. This time he was to voyage southward for that passage named after Juan de Fuca. This would lead him north of Drake's New Albion in California, and north of the Spanish cruisings about modern Vancouver Island. This was to bring him to the mythical Gamaland. Bering knew there was no Gamaland; but in the captain's cabin, where the savants bent all day over charts, was the map of Delisle, the geographer of French Canada, showing vast unnamed lands north of the Spanish possessions; and in the expedition was a member of the Delisle family. So Bering must have known or guessed that an empire half the size of Russia lay undiscovered north of Juan de Fuca's passage.

So confident were the members of the expedition of reaching land to the east at an early date that provisions and water for only a few weeks were carried along. Bering had a crew of seventy-seven on the *St. Peter*, and among the other men of science with him was the famous naturalist, George W. Steller. Lieutenant Chirikoff sailed the *St. Paul* with seventy-six men, and Delisle de la Croyère was his most distinguished passenger. As is usual during early June in that latitude, driving rains and dense fogs came rolling down from the north over a choppy sea. The fog turned to snow, and the *St. Paul*, far in the lead, came about to signal if they should not keep together to avoid losing each other in the thick weather; but the *St. Peter* was careening dangerously, and shipping thunderous seas astern. Bering's laconic signal in answer was to keep on south 'to Gamaland'; but when the fog lifted the *St. Peter* was in latitude 46°, far below the supposed location of the strait of Juan de Fuca, and there was in sight neither Gamaland nor the sister ship. The scientists with Bering were in such a peevish mood over the utter disproof of their mythical continent that they insisted on the commander wasting a whole month pottering back and forth looking for Chirikoff's ship. By this time the weather had become very warm, the drinking water very rank, and the provisions stale. Finally, the learned men gave decision that as the other ship could not be found the *St. Peter* might as well turn north.

Bering had become very depressed, and so irritable that he could not tolerate approach. If the men of learning had been but wise in the dangers of ocean travel, they would have recognized in their commander the symptoms of the common sea-scourge of the age— scurvy. Presently, he was too ill to leave his bed, and Waxel, who hated all interference and threatened to put the scientists in irons or throw them overboard, took command. By the middle of July passengers and crew were reduced to half allowance of bad water. Still, there were signs that afforded hope. As the ship worked through the fog-blanket northward, drift-wood and land birds, evidently from a land other than Asia, were seen.

At last came a land wind from the southeast, lifting the fog and driving it back to the north. And early one morning there were confused cries from the deck hands—then silence—then shouts of exultant joy! Everybody rushed above-decks, even the sick in their night-robes, among them Bering, wan and weak, answering scarce a word to the happy clamour about him. Before the sailors' astonished gaze, in the very early light of that northern latitude, lay a turquoise sea—a shining sheet of water, milky and metallic like a mountain tarn, with the bright greens and blues of glacial silt; and looming through the primrose clouds of the horizon hung a huge opal dome in mid-heaven. At first they hardly realized what it meant. Then shouts went up—'Land!' 'Mountains!' 'Snowpeaks!' The *St. Peter* glided forward noiseless as a bird on the wing. Inlets and harbours, turquoise-green and silent, opened along a jagged, green and alabaster shore. As the vessel approached the land the explorers saw that the white wall of the inner harbour was a rampart of solid ice; but where the shore line extended out between ice and sea was a meadow of ferns and flowers abloom knee-deep, and grasses waist-high. The spectators shouted and laughed and cried and embraced one another. Russia, too, had found a new empire. St. Elias they named the great peak that hung like a temple dome of marble above the lesser ridges; but Bering only sighed. 'We think we have done great things, eh? Well, who knows where this is? We're almost out of provisions, and not a man of us knows which way to sail home.'

Steller was down the ship's ladder with the glee of a schoolboy, and off for the shore with fifteen men in one of the row-boats to explore. They found the dead ashes of a camp-fire on the sands, and some remnants of smoked fish; but any hope that the lost ship's crew had camped here was at once dispelled by the print of moccasined feet in the fine sand. Steller found some rude huts covered with sea-moss, but no human presence. Water-casks were filled; and that relieved a pressing need. On July 21, when the wind began to blow freshly seaward, Bering appeared unexpectedly on deck, ashen of hue and staggering from weakness, and peremptorily ordered anchors up. Bells were rung and gongs beaten to call those ashore back to the ship. Steller stormed and swore. Was it for this hurried race ashore that he had spent years toiling across two continents? He wanted to botanize, to explore, to gather data for science; but the commander had had enough of science. He was sick unto death, in body and in soul, sick with the knowledge that they were two thousand miles from any known port, in a tempestuous sea, on a rickety ship manned for the most part by land-lubbers.

As they scudded before the wind, Bering found that the shore was trending south towards the home harbour. They were following that long line of reefed islands, the Aleutians, which project out from Alaska towards Asia. A roar of reefs through the fog warned them off the land; but one midnight of August the lead recorded less than three feet of water under the keel. Before there was time for panic, a current that rushed between rocks threw the vessel into a deep pool of backwash; and there she lay till morning. By this time many of the sailors were down with scurvy. It became necessary to land for fresh water. One man died as he was lifted from the decks to the shore. Bering could not stand unaided. Twenty emaciated sailors were taken out of their berths and propped up on the sand. And the water they took from this rocky island was brackish, and only increased the ravages of the malady.

From the date of this ill-fated landing, a pall—a state of paralysis, of inaction and fear—seemed to hang over the ship. The tide-rip was mistaken for earthquake; and when the lurid glare of volcanic smoke came through the fog, the sailors huddled panic-stricken below-decks and refused to obey orders. Every man became his own master; and if that ever works well on land, it means disaster at sea. Thus it has almost always been with the inefficient and the misfits who have gone out in ships—land-lubbers trying to be navigators. Just when Bering's crew should have braced themselves to resist the greatest stress, they collapsed and huddled together with bowed heads, inviting the worst that fate could do to them. When the tiderip came through the reefs from the north along the line of the Aleutian Islands with the swiftness of a mill-race, the men had literally to be held to the rudder at pistol point and beaten up the masts with the flat of the officers' swords. But while they skulked, a hurricane rolled up the fog; and the ship could but scud under bare poles before the wind. Rations were now down to mouldy sea-biscuits, and only fifteen casks of water remained for three-score men.

Out of the turmoil of waters and wind along the wave-lashed rocks came the hoarse, shrill, strident cry of the sea-lion, the boom and snort of the great walrus, the roar of the seal rookeries, where millions of cubs wallowed, and where bulls lashed themselves in their rage and fought for mastery of the herd. By November, Waxel alone was holding the vessel up to the wind. No more solemn conferences of self-important, self-willed scientists filled the commander's cabin. No more solemn conclaves and arguments and counterarguments to induce the commander to sail this way and that! Bedlam reigned above and below decks. No man had any thought but how to reach home alive. Prayers and vows and offerings went up from the decks of the *St. Peter* like smoke. The Russians vowed themselves to holy lives and stopped swearing.

To the inexpressible delight of all hands the prayers seemed to be heard. On November 4 the storm abated, and land loomed up on the horizon, dim at first, but taking shape as the vessel approached it and showing a well-defined, rock-bound harbour. Was this the home harbour? The sick crawled on hands and knees above the hatchway to mumble out their thanks to God for escape from doom. A cask of brandy was opened, and tears gave place to gruff, hilarious laughter. Every man was ready to swear that he recognized this headland, that he had known they were following the right course after all, and that he had never felt any fear at all.

Barely had the grief become joy, when a chill silence fell over the ship. The only sounds were the rattling of the rigging against the masts, the groaning of the timbers of the vessel, and the swish of the waves cut by the prow. These were not Kamchatka shores. This was only another of the endless island reefs they had been chasing since July. The tattered sails flapped and beat dismally against the cordage. Night fell. There was a retributive glee in the whistle of the mocking wind through the rotten rigging, and the ship's timbers groaned to the boom of the heavy tide.

Bering was past caring whether he lived or died. Morning revealed a shore of black basalt, reef upon reef, like sentinels of death saying, 'Come in! come in! We are here to see that you never go out'; and there was a nasty clutch to the backwash of the billows smashing down from those rocks.

Waxel called a last council of all hands in the captain's cabin. 'We should go on home,' said Bering, rising on his elbow in his berth. 'It matters not to me. I am past mending; but even if we have only the foremast left and one keg of water, let us try for the home harbour. A few days must make it. Having risked so much, let us risk all to win!' As they afterwards found, they were only one week from Kamchatka; but they were terrified at the prospect of any more deep-sea wanderings, and when one of the officers dared to support Bering's view, they fell on him like wild beasts and threw him from the cabin. To a man they voted to land. That vote was fate's seal to the penalty men must pay for their mistakes.

Above the white fret of reefs precipices towered in pinnacles two thousand feet high. Through the reefs the doomed ship stole like a hunted thing. Only one man kept his head clear and his hand to the helm—the lieutenant whom all the rest had thrown out of the cabin. The island seemed absolutely treeless, covered only with sedge and shingle and grass. The tide began to toss the ship about so that the sick were rolled from their berths. Night came with a ghostly moonlight silvering the fret of a seething sea that seemed to be reaching up white arms for its puny victims. The lieutenant threw out an anchor. It raked bottom and the cable snapped. The crazed crew began throwing the dead overboard as an offering to appease the anger of the sea. The *St. Peter* swept stern foremost full on a reef. Quickly the lieutenant and Steller threw out the last anchor. It gripped between rocks and—held. The tide at midnight had thrown the vessel into a sheltered cove. Steller and the lieutenant at once rowed ashore to examine their surroundings and to take steps to make provision for the morrow. They were on what is now known as Bering Island. Fortunately, it was literally swarming with animal life—the great manatee or sea-cow in herds on the kelp-beds, blue foxes in thousands, the seal rookeries that were to make the islands famous; but there was no timber to build houses for wintering in. It was a barren island. They could make floors of sand, walls of peat, roofs of sea-moss; but what shelter was this against northern gales?

By November 8 a rude pit-shelter had been constructed to house the invalided crew; but the sudden transition from the putrid hold to the open, frosty air caused the death of many as they were lowered on stretchers. Amid a heavy snow Bering was wrapped in furs and carried ashore. The dauntless Steller faced the situation with judgment and courage. He acted as doctor, nurse, and hunter, and daily brought in meat for the hungry and furs to cover the dying. Five pits sheltered the castaways. When examined in 1885 the walls of the pits were still intact—three feet of solid peat. Clothing of sea-otter skins of priceless value, which afterwards proved a fortune to those who survived, and food of the flesh of the great sea-cow, saved a remnant of the wretched crew. During most of the month of November the

St. Peter rode safely at anchor while storms thundered around her retreat; but on the 28th her cable snapped beneath a hurricane, and she was driven high and dry on the shore, a broken wreck. In all thirty-one men had perished of scurvy by January 1742. Among these was the poor old commander. On the morning of December 8, as the wind went moaning round their shelter, Steller heard the Dane praying in a low voice. And just at daybreak he passed into that great, quiet Unknown World whence no traveller has returned.

How the consort ship, the *St. Paul*, found her way back to Kamchatka, and how Bering's castaways in the spring built themselves a raft and mustered their courage to essay the voyage home which they ought to have attempted in the autumn, are matters for more detailed history. But just as Cartier's discovery of the St. Lawrence led to the pursuit of the little beaver across a continent, so the Russians' discovery of Alaska and the Aleutian Islands led to the pursuit of the sea-otter up and down the North Pacific; led the way, indeed, to that contest for world supremacy on the Pacific in which the great powers of three continents are to-day engaged.

THE OUTLAW HUNTERS

Chirikoff's crew on the *St. Paul* had long since returned in safety to Kamchatka, and the garrison of the fort on Avacha Bay had given up Bering's men as lost for ever, when one August morning the sentinel on guard along the shore front of Petropavlovsk descried a strange apparition approaching across the silver surface of an unruffled sea. It was like a huge whale, racing, galloping, coming in leaps and bounds of flying fins over the water towards the fort. The soldier telescoped his eyes with his hands and looked again. This was no whale. There was a mast pole with a limp skin-thing for sail. It was a big, clumsy, raft-shaped flat-boat. The oarsmen were rowing like pursued maniacs, rising and falling bodily as they pulled. It was this that gave the craft the appearance of galloping over the water. The soldier called down others to look. Some one ran for the commander of the fort. What puzzled the onlookers was the appearance of the rowers. They did not look like human beings; their hair was long; their beards were unkempt. They were literally naked except for breech-clouts and shoulder-pieces of fur. Then somebody shouted the unexpected tidings that they were the castaways of Bering's crew.

Bugles rang; the fort drum rumbled a muster; the chapel bells pealed forth; and the whole population of the fort rushed to the water-side—shouting, gesticulating, laughing, crying—and welcomed with wild embraces the returning castaways. And while men looked for this one and that among the two-score coming ashore from the raft, and women wept for those they did not find, on the outskirts of the crowd stood silent observers—Chinese traders and pedlars from Manchuria, who yearly visited Kamchatka to gather pelts for the annual great fur fairs held in China. The Chinese merchants looked hard; then nodded knowingly to each other, and came furtively down amid the groups along the shore front and timidly fingered the matted pelts worn by the half-naked men. It was incredible. Each penniless castaway was wearing the fur of the sea-otter, or what the Russians called the sea-beaver, more valuable than seal, and, even at that day, rarer than silver fox. Never suspecting their value, the castaways had brought back a great number of the pelts of these animals; and when the Chinese merchants paid over the value of these furs in gold, the Russians awakened to a realization that while Bering had not found a Gamaland, he might have stumbled on as great a source of wealth as the furs of French Canada or the gold-lined temples of Peru.

The story Bering's men told was that, while searching ravenously for food on the barren island where they had been cast, they had found vast kelp-beds and seaweed marshes, where pastured the great manatee known as the sea-cow. Its flesh had saved their lives. While hunting the sea-cow in the kelp-beds and sea-marshes the men had noticed that whenever a swashing sea or tide drove the shattering spray up the rocks, there would come riding in on the storm whole herds of another sea denizen—thousands upon thousands of them, so tame that they did not know the fear of man, burying their heads in the sea-kelp while the storm raged, lifting them only to breathe at intervals. This creature was six feet long from the tip of its round, cat-shaped nose to the end of its stumpy, beaver-shaped tail, with fur the colour of ebony on the surface, soft seal-colour and grey below, and deep as sable. Quite unconscious of the worth of the fur, the castaway sailors fell on these visitors to the kelp-beds and clubbed right and left, for skins to protect their nakedness from the biting winter winds.

It was the news of the sea wealth brought to Kamchatka by Bering's men that sent traders scurrying to the Aleutian Islands and Alaskan shores. Henceforth Siberian merchants were to vie with each other in outfitting hunters—criminals, political exiles, refugees, destitute sailors—to scour the coasts of America for sea-otter. Throughout the long line of the Aleutian Islands and the neighbouring coasts of North America, for over a century, hunters' boats—little cockle-shell skiffs made of oiled walrus-skin stretched on whalebone frames, narrow as a canoe, light as cork—rode the wildest seas in the wildest storms in pursuit of the sea-otter. Sea-otter became to the Pacific coast what beaver was to the Atlantic—the magnet that drew traders to the north-west seas, and ultimately led to the settlement of the north-west coast.

It was, to be sure, dangerous work hunting in wild northern gales on rocks slippery with ice and through spray that wiped out every outline of precipice edge or reef; but it offered variety to exiles in Siberia; and it offered more—a chance of wealth if they survived. Iron for bolts of boats must be brought all the way from Europe; so the outlaw hunters did without iron, and fastened planks together as best they could with deer thongs in place of nails, and moss and tallow in place of tar. In the crazy vessels so constructed they ventured out from Kamchatka two thousand miles across unknown boisterous seas. Once they had reached the Aleutians, natives were engaged to do the actual hunting under their direction. Exiles and criminals could not be expected to use gentle methods to attain their ends. 'God is high in the heavens and the Czar is far away,' they said. The object was quick profit, and plundering was the easiest way to attain it. How were the Aleutian Indians paid? At first they were not paid at all. They were drugged into service with vodka, a liquor that put them in a frenzy; and bayoneted and bludgeoned into obedience. These methods failing, wives and children were seized by the Russians and held in camp as hostages to guarantee a big hunt. The Aleuts' one object in meeting the Russian hunter at all was to get possession of firearms. From the time Bering's crew and Chirikoff's men had first fired rifles in the presence of these poor savages of the North, the Indians had realized that 'the stick that thundered' was a weapon they must possess, or see their tribe exterminated.

The brigades of sea-otter hunters far exceeded in size and wild daring the platoons of beaver hunters, who ranged by pack-horse and canoe from Hudson Bay to the Rocky Mountains. The Russian ship, provisioned for two or three years, would moor and draw up ashore for the winter on one of the eleven hundred Aleutian Islands. Huts would be constructed of drift-wood, roofed with sea-moss; and as time went on even rude forts were erected on two or three of the islands—like Oonalaska or Kadiak—where the kelp-beds were extensive and the hunting was good enough to last for several years. The Indians would then be attracted to the camp by presents of brandy and glass beads and gay trinkets and firearms. Perhaps one thousand Aleut hunters would be assembled. Two types of hunting boats were used—the big 'bidarkie,' carrying twenty or thirty men, and the little kayak, a mere cockle-shell. Oiled walrus-skin, stretched taut as a drum-head, served as a covering for the kayak against the seas, a manhole being left in the centre for the paddler to ensconce himself waist-deep, with oilskin round his waist to keep the water out. Clothing was worn fur side in, oiled side out; and the soles of all moccasins were padded with moss to protect the feet from the sharp rocks. Armed with clubs, spears, steel gaffs and rifles, the hunters would paddle out into the storm.

There were three types of hunting—long distance rifle-shooting, which the Russians taught the Aleuts; still hunting in a calm sea; storm hunting on the kelp-beds and rocks as the wild tide rode in with its myriad swimmers. Rifles could be used only when the wind was away from the sea-otter beds and the rocks offered good hiding above the sea-swamps. This method was sea-otter hunting *de luxe*. Still hunting could only be followed when the sea was smooth as glass. The Russian schooner would launch out a brigade of cockle-shell kayaks on an unruffled stretch of sea, which the sea-otter traversed going to and from the kelp-beds. While the sea-otter is a marine denizen, it must come up to breathe; and if it does not come up frequently of its own volition, the gases forming in its body bring it to the surface. The little kayaks would circle out silent as shadows over the silver surface of the sea. A round head would bob up, or a bubble show where a swimmer was moving below the sur-face. The kayaks would narrow their surrounding circle. Presently a head would appear. The hunter nearest would deal the death-stroke with his steel gaff, and the quarry would be drawn in. But it was in the storm hunt over the kelp-beds that the wildest work went on. Through the fiercest storm scudded bidarkies and kayaks, meeting the herds of sea-otter as they drove before the gale. To be sure, the bidarkies filled and foundered; the kayaks were ripped on the teeth of the rock reefs. But the sea took no account of its dead; neither did the Russians. Only the Aleut women and children wept for the loss of the hunters who never returned; and sea-otter hunting decreased the population of the Aleutian Islands by thousands. It was as fatal to the Indian as to the sea-otter. Two hundred thousand sea-otters were taken by the Russians in half a century. Kadiak yielded as many as 6000 pelts in a single year; Oonalaska, 3000; the Pribylovs, 5000; Sitka used to yield 15,000 a year. To-day there are barely 200 a year found from the Commander Islands to Sitka.

It may be imagined that Russian criminals were not easy masters to the simple Aleut women and children who were held as hostages in camp to guarantee a good hunt. Brandy flowed like water, the Czar was far away, and it was a land with no law but force. The Russian hunters cast conscience and fear to the winds. Who could know? God did not seem to see; and it was two thousand miles to the home fort in Kamchatka. When the hunt was poor, children were brained with clubbed rifles, women knouted to death before the eyes of husbands and fathers. In 1745 a whole village of Aleuts had poison put in their food by the Russians. The men were to eat first, and when they perished the women and children would be left as slaves to the Russians. A Cossack, Pushkareff, brought a ship out for the merchant Betshevin in 1762, and, in punishment for the murder of several brutal members of the crew by the Aleuts, he kidnapped twenty-five of their women. Then, as storm drove him towards Kamchatka, he feared to enter the home port with such a damning human cargo. So he promptly marooned fourteen victims on a rocky coast, and binding the others hand and foot, threw them into the sea. The merchant and the Cossack were both finally punished by the Russian government for the crimes of this voyage; but this did not silence the blood of the murdered women crying to Heaven for vengeance. In September 1762 the criminal ship came back to Avacha Bay. In complete ignorance of the Cossack's diabolical conduct, four Russian ships sailed that very month for the Aleutian Islands. Since 1741, when Bering's sailors had found the kelp-beds, Aleuts had hunted the sea-otter and Russians had hunted the Aleuts. For three years fate reversed the wheel. It was to be a man-hunt of fugitive Russians.

Just before the snow fell in the autumn of 1763 Alexis Drusenin anchored his ship on the north-east corner of Oonalaska, where the rocks sprawl out in the sea in five great spurs like the fingers of a hand. The spurs are separated by tempestuous reef-ribbed seas. The Indians were so very friendly that they voluntarily placed hostages of good conduct in the Russians' hands. Two or three thousand Aleut hunters came flocking over the sea in their kayaks to join the sea-otter brigades. On the spur opposite to Drusenin's anchorage stood an Aleut village of forty houses; on the next spur, ten miles away across the sea, was another village of seventy people. The Russian captain divided his crew, and placed from nine to twelve men in each of the villages. With ample firearms and enough brandy half a dozen Russians could control a thousand Aleuts. Swaggering and bullying and loud-voiced and pot-valiant, Drusenin and two Cossacks stooped to enter a low-thatched Aleut hut. The entrance step pitched down into a sort of pit; and as Drusenin stumbled in face foremost a cudgel clubbed down on his skull. The Cossack behind stumbled headlong over the prostrate form of his officer; and in the dark there was a flash of long knives—such knives as the hunters used in skinning their prey. Both bodies were cut to fragments. The third man seized an axe as the murderers crowded round him and beat them back; he then sought safety in flight. There was a hiss of hurtling spears thrown after him with terrible deftness. With his back pierced in a dozen places, drenched in his own blood, the Cossack almost tumbled over the prostrate body of a sentinel who had been on guard at a house down by the ship, and had been wounded by the flying spears. A sailor dashed out, a yard-long bear-knife in his grasp, and dragged the two men inside. Of the dozen Russians stationed here only four survived; and their hut was beset by a rabble of Aleuts drunk with vodka, drunk with blood, drunk with a frenzy of revenge.

Cooped up in the hut, the Russians kept guard by twos till nightfall, when, dragging a 'bidarkie' down to the water, they loaded it with provisions and firearms, and pushed out in the dark to the moan and heave of an unquiet sea. Though weakened from loss of blood, the fugitives rowed with fury for the next spur of rock, ten miles away, where they hoped to find help. The tide-rip came out of the north with angry threat and broke against the rocks, but no blink of light shone through the dark from the Russian huts ashore. The men were afraid to land, and afraid not to land. Wind and sea would presently crush their frail craft to kindling-wood against the rocky shore.

The Russians sprang out, waded ashore, uttered a shout. Instantly lances and spears fell about them like rain. They joined hands and ran for the cove where the big schooner had been moored. Breathlessly they waited for the dawn to discover where their ship lay; but daylight revealed only the broken wreckage of the vessel along the shore, while all about were blood-stains and pieces of clothing and mutilated bodies, which told but too plainly that the crew had been hacked to pieces. There was not a moment to be lost. Before the mist could lift, the fugitives gathered up some provisions scattered on the shore and ran for their lives to the high mountains farther inland. And when daylight came they scooped a hole in the sand, drew a piece of sail-cloth over this, and lay in hiding till night.

From early December to early February the Russians hid in the caves of the Oonalaska mountains. Clams, shell-fish, sea-birds stayed their hunger. It is supposed that they must have found shelter in one of the caves where there are medicinal hot springs; otherwise, they would have perished of cold. In February they succeeded in making a rude boat, and in this they set out by night to seek the ships of other Russian hunters. For a week they rowed out only at night. Then they began to row by day. They were seen by Indians, and once more sought safety in the caves of the mountains, where they remained in hiding for five weeks, venturing out only at night in search of food. Here, snow-water and shell-fish were all they had to sustain them; and again they must build a rude raft to escape. Towards the end of March they descried a Russian vessel in the offing, and at last succeeded in reaching friends.

Almost the same story could be told of the crews of each of the ships that had sailed from Avacha Bay in September 1762. One ship foundered. The castaways were stabbed where they lay in exhausted sleep. Every member of the crew on a third ship had been slain round a bath-house, such as Russian hunters built in that climate to enable them to ward off rheumatism by vapour plunges. One ship only escaped the general butchery and carried the refugees home.

Of course, Cossack and hunter exacted terrible vengeance for this massacre. Whole villages were burned to the ground and every inhabitant sabred. On one occasion, as many as three hundred victims were tied in line and shot. The result was that the Cossacks' outrages and the Aleuts' vengeance drew the attention of the Russian government to this lucrative fur trade in the far new land. The disorders put an end to free, unrestricted trade. Henceforth a hunter must have a licence; and a licence implied the favour of the court. The court saw to it that a governor took up his residence in the region to enforce justice and to compel the hunters to make honest returns. Like the Hudson's Bay men, the Russian fur traders had to report direct to the crown. Thus was inaugurated on the west coast of America the Russian régime, which ended only in 1867, when Alaska was ceded to the United States.

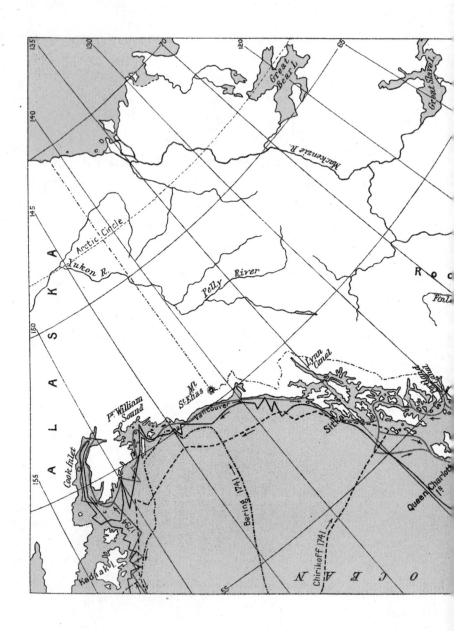

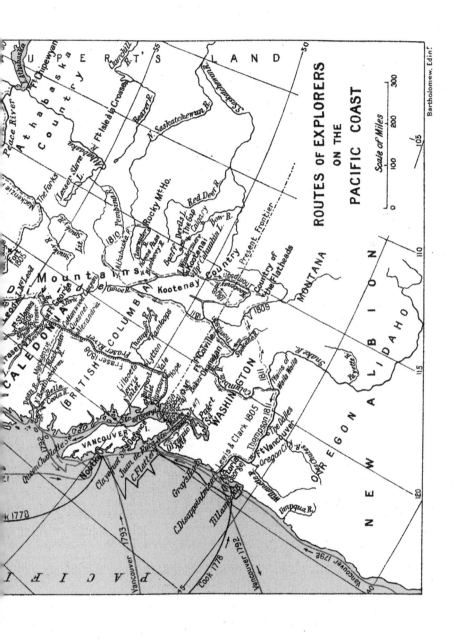

COOK AND VANCOUVER

It was the quest for a passage to the Atlantic that brought Captain James Cook to the Pacific. Before joining the Royal Navy, Cook had been engaged as a captain in the Baltic trade; and from Russian merchantmen he had learned all about Bering's voyage in the North Pacific, which was being quoted by the geographers in proof of an open passage north of Alaska. In the Baltic, too, Cook had heard about the strait of Juan de Fuca, which was supposed to lead through the continent to the Atlantic. At this time all England was agog with demands that the Hudson's Bay Company should find a North-West Passage or surrender its charter. Parliament had offered a reward of £20,000 to any one discovering a passage-way to the Pacific, and Samuel Hearne had been sent tramping inland to explore the north by land. Curiously enough, Cook had been born in 1728, the very year that Bering had set out on his first expedition; and he was in the Baltic when news came back to St. Petersburg of Bering's death. The year 1759 found him at Quebec with Wolfe. During the next ten years he explored and charted northern and southern seas; and when the British parliament determined to set at rest for ever the myth of a passage, Cook was chosen to conduct the expedition. He was granted two ships—the

Resolution and the *Discovery*; and among the crews was a young midshipman named Vancouver. The vessels left England in the summer of 1776, and sailed from the Sandwich Islands in 1778 for Drake's New Albion. The orders were to proceed from New Albion up to 65° north latitude and search for a passage to Hudson Bay.

On March 7, 1778—two hundred years after Drake's famous voyage—Cook's ships descried thin, sharp lines of land in the offing. As the vessels drew nearer the coast towering mountains met the gaze of the explorers. Cook had orders to keep a sharp look-out in this region for the strait of Juan de Fuca; but storm drove him off-shore, and, although he discovered and named Cape Flattery at the entrance to the strait that now bears the name. From the portrait by Dance in the Gallery of Greenwich Hospital of the old Greek pilot, he did not catch as much as a glimpse of the great bay opening inland. In fact, he set down that in this latitude there was no possibility of Juan de Fuca's strait existing. Landing was made on Vancouver Island at the famous harbour now known as Nootka; and Indians swarmed the sea in gaily painted dug-outs with prows carved like totem-poles. Women and children were in the canoes. That signified peace; and though cannon were manned in readiness, an active and friendly trade at once opened between the crews and the natives. Fifteen hundred beaver and sea-otter pelts were exchanged for a handful of old nails. At least two thousand natives gathered round the two ships. Some of the men wore masks and had evidently just returned from a raid, for they offered Cook human skulls from which the flesh had not been removed, and pointed to slave captives.

Any one who knows Vancouver Island in spring needs no description of the inspiring scene surveyed by the sea-weary crews. Snow rested on the coastal mountains. The huge opal dome now known as Mount Baker loomed up through the clouds of dawn and dusk on the southern sky-line. In fair weather the long pink ridge of the Olympics could be seen towards Puget Sound. Inland from Nootka were vast mountain ridges heavily forested to the very clouds with fir trees and spruce of incredible size. Lower down grew cypress, with gnarled red roots entangling the rocks to the very water's edge, Spanish moss swinging from branch to branch, and partridge drumming in the underbrush. For a month the deep-sea travellers enjoyed a welcome furlough on shore. One night the underbrush surrounding the encampment was found to be literally alive with painted warriors. Cook demanded an explanation of the grand 'tyee' or chief. The Indian explained that these were guards to protect the encampment. However that might be, Cook deemed it well to be off.

On May 1 the ships were skirting the Sitka coast, which Chirikoff and Bering had explored a quarter of a century previously. St. Elias, Bering's landfall, was sighted. So was the spider-shaped bay now known as Prince William Sound. The Indians here resembled the Eskimos of Greenland so strongly that the hopes of the explorers began to rise. So keen were they to prove the existence of a passage to the Atlantic that when swords, beads, powder, evidently obtained from white traders, were observed among the Indians, the Englishmen tried to persuade themselves that these Indians must be in communication with the Indians of the domain of the Hudson's Bay Company, forgetting that Russians had been on the ground for forty years. Cook sailed round the coast, past Cape Prince of Wales and through Bering Strait, keeping his prows northward until an impassable wall of ice barred his way. Having now thoroughly explored the coast, Cook was satisfied that Drake and Bering had been right. There was no passage east. He then crossed to Siberia, sailed down the Asiatic coast, and visited the Aleutian Islands. The Russians of Oonalaska and Kamchatka resented the English intrusion on their hunting-ground, while the English refused to acknowledge that they were invading Russian territory.

It was planned to winter and repair the ships at the Sandwich Islands. This part of Cook's voyage does not concern Canada. It was something like a repetition of the transgressions of the Russian outlaw hunters, and was followed by the penalty that transgressors pay. The islanders had welcomed the white men as demi-gods, but the gods so proved to have feet of clay. To the islanders a sacred 'taboo' always existed round the burial-graves. Cook permitted his sailors to violate this 'taboo' in order to take timber for the repair of his ships. Perhaps it was a reaction from almost three years of navy discipline; perhaps it was the influence of those seductive southern seas; however that may be, the sailors apparently gave themselves up to riotous debauch. The best of the islanders withdrew disillusioned, sad, sullen, resentful over the violation of their sacred burial-places. Only the riff-raff of the natives forgathered with the riotous crew. When the ships at length set sail with a crew sore-headed from dissipation, by way of a climax to the debauch, a number of women and children were carried along.

Retribution came swift as sword-stroke. The women set up such a wailing that Cook stopped the ships to set them ashore. In the delay of rowing the boats to land a fierce gale sprang up. The wind snapped off the foremast of the *Resolution* clean to the decks. The two ships had to put back to the harbour for repairs. Not a canoe, not a man, not a voice, welcomed them. The sailors were sullen; Cook was angry; and when the white men wanted to trade for fresh food, the islanders would take only daggers and knives in barter. The white men had stolen from their burial-graves. The savages now tried to steal from the ships, and on Sunday, February 14, they succeeded in carrying off the large row-boat of the *Discovery*.

Cook landed with a strong bodyguard to demand hostages for the return of the lost boat. The islanders remembered the kidnapping of the women, and refused. Cook was foolhardy enough to order his men to fire on any canoe trying to escape from the harbour. The rest of the episode is so familiar that it scarcely needs telling. A chief crossing the harbour in a skiff was shot. The women were at once hurried off to the hills. The men donned their spears and war-mats. A stone hurled from the rabble running down to the shore struck Cook. Enraged out of all self-control, he shot the culprit dead.

James Cook.
FROM THE PORTRAIT BY DANCE IN THE
GALLERY OF GREENWICH HOSPITAL

In defence of their commander some marines rowing ashore at once fired a musketry volley into the horde of islanders. Cook turned his back to the thronging savages, now frenzied to a delirium, and signalled the marines to cease firing. As he did so, a dagger was plunged beneath his shoulder-blade. He was hacked to pieces under the eyes of his powerless men; and four soldiers also fell beneath the furious onslaught.

What need to tell of the wild scramble for the sea; of the war-horns blowing all night in the dark; of the camp-fires glimmering from the women's retreat in the hills? By dint of threat and show of arms and promises, Captain Charles Clerke, who was now in command, induced the islanders to deliver the remnants of Cook's body. In an impressive silence, on Sunday the 21st of February 1779, the coffin containing the great commander's bones was committed to the deep.

The sensational nature of Cook's death, within half a century of Bering's equally tragic fate, while exploring the same unknown seas, spread round the world the fame of the exploits of both. It was recalled that Drake had claimed New Albion for England two centuries before. Then rumours came that the Spanish viceroy in Mexico had been following up the discoveries of both Drake and Bering. One Bruno Heceta from Monterey made report that there were signs of a great turbid river cutting the coast-line north of Drake's New Albion. In spite of Cook's adverse report, the questions were again mooted: Where was Juan de Fuca's strait? Did it lead to Hudson Bay? Where was this Great River of which both the inland savages and the Spanish explorers spoke? Quebec had fallen. Scottish fur merchants of Montreal had formed the North-West Company in opposition to the Hudson's Bay Company, and were pushing their traders far west towards the Rockies, far north towards the Arctic Circle. Who would be first to find the great unknown river, to fathom the mysteries of Juan de Fuca's strait? Dreaming of these things up in the Athabaska country, Alexander Mackenzie, a trader for the Nor'westers, was preparing to push his canoes down to the Arctic as a preliminary to his greater journey to the Pacific. If Bering's crew, if Cook's crew, both sold half-rotted cargoes of furs for thousands of pounds, how much more easily could trading vessels properly equipped reap fortune from the new El Dorado!

Inland by canoe from Montreal, overland by flat-boat and pack-horse from the Missouri, across the continent from Hudson Bay, round the world by the Cape and the Horn, across the ocean from China—it now became a race to the Pacific. Greater wealth seemed there in furs than had been found in gold in the temples of Peru, or in silver in the mines of Mexico. The struggle for control of the Pacific, which has culminated in our own day, now began. Spain, Russia, England, Canada, and the new-born United States were the contestants in the arena. What has reached its climax in the sluicing of two oceans together at Panama began in the pursuit of sea-otter and seal after the voyages of Bering and of Cook.

The United States had an added motive. On the principle of protecting native shipping, American ports discriminated against British ships, and British ports discriminated against American ships. It was absolutely necessary to their existence as a nation that the United States should build up a merchant fleet. Under fostering laws, with the advantages of cheap labour and abundant timber, a wonderful clipper fleet had been constructed in Massachusetts and Maryland and Virginia ship-yards, consisting of swift sailing-vessels suitable for belting the seas in promoting commerce and in war. The ship-yards built on shares with the merchants, who outfitted the cargo. Builders and merchants would then divide the profits. Under these conditions American traders were penetrating almost every sea in the world; and the cargoes brought back built up the substantial fortunes of many old Boston families. 'Bostonnais' these swift new traders were called from

the Baltic to China. It can be readily believed that what they heard of
Cook and Bering interested the Boston men mightily. At all events,
they fitted out two ships for the Pacific trade—ships that were to
range the seas for the United States as Drake's and Cook's had drawn
a circle round the world for England. Captain John Kendrick commanded the *Columbia*, Captain Robert Gray the *Lady Washington*,
and on one of the vessels was a sailor who had been to the North-
West coast with Cook. In order to secure Spain's goodwill, letters were
obtained to the viceroy of Mexico; and when, in the course of the
voyage, these letters were presented to the viceroy of Mexico at San
Blas, he honoured them by at once issuing orders to the presidios of
Monterey and Santa Barbara and San Francisco to arrest both officers
and crew if the Americans touched at any Spanish port. Spain was still
dreaming of the Pacific being 'a closed sea.' She took cognizance of
Bering's exploits to the north, but she at once strove to checkmate an
advance south from the north, by herself advancing north from the
south. It was in 1775 that Heceta had observed the turbid entrance
to a great river and the opening to a strait that might be that of Juan
de Fuca. However, on Monday, October 1, 1787, the two American
vessels sailed away from Boston. It was August of 1788 before they
were off Drake's New Albion; and in the stormy weather encountered
all the way up the Pacific, the little sloop *Lady Washington* had proved
a faster, better sailer than the heavier cargo vessel, the *Columbia*.
Signs of a river were observed; and a pause was made at one of the
harbours on the coast—either Tillamook or Gray's Harbour. Here the
Indians, indignant at a recent outrage committed against them by
whites, attacked the Americans and drove them off before they could
search for an entrance to the Great River. It now became apparent
that the small sloop had the advantage, not only in speed, but because
it could go in closer to the coast. Towards the end of August Gray's
crew distinctly observed the Olympic mountains and set down record
of Cape Flattery. 'I am of opinion,' notes the mate, 'that the Straits of
Juan de Fuca *do* exist; for the coast takes a great bend here.'

At Nootka surprise awaited the Americans. John Meares and William Douglas, English captains, were there in a palisaded fort and with two vessels; a little trading schooner of thirty tons named the *North-West America* had just been built—the first ship built on the North-West coast—and was being launched amid thunder of cannon and clinking of glasses, and September 19 was observed as a holiday—the first public holiday in what is now British Columbia. Meares and Douglas entertained Gray at dinner, and over brimming wine-glasses gave him the news of recent happenings on the coast. Captain Barkley, another English trader, had looked into the Strait of Juan de Fuca and placed it on his chart. Meares had sought in vain for the River of the West, and did not believe that it existed. In fact, he had named the headland that hid it Cape Disappointment. And, of course, no furs existed on the Pacific coast. When did a fur trader ever acknowledge to a rival that there were furs? Meares reported that he, too, had been down at Tillamook Bay; and Gray guessed that it had been Meares's injustice to the Indians that provoked the raid on himself. Meares was short of provisions, and the *Lady Washington* needed repairs. The American gave the Englishman provisions to reach China, and the Englishman repaired the American's ship. Meares declared that he had bought all Nootka from the Indians. He did not relate that he had paid only two pocket-pistols and some copper for it. Towards the end of September came Kendrick on the belated *Columbia*. Both Americans were surprised to learn that half a dozen navigators had already gone as far north as Nootka Sound. Perez, Heceta, Quadra—all had coasted Vancouver Island for Spain from 1774 to 1779, and so had La Pérouse, the French explorer, in 1787. Hanna had come out from China for furs in 1785. In 1787 Portlock and Dixon had secured almost two thousand sea-otter skins as far north as the Queen Charlotte Islands. These were things Meares did not tell the Americans. It would have been to acknowledge that an abundance of furs was there to draw so many trading-ships. But during the winter at Nootka the men from Boston learned these facts from the Indians.

The launch of the *North-West America* at Nootka Sound, 1788.
FROM MEARES'S *VOYAGES*

The winter was passed in trading with the Indians, and spring saw Gray far up the Strait of Juan de Fuca. By May 1 the ships were loaded with furs and were about to sail. Meanwhile, what had the Spanish viceroy been doing? Strange that the Spaniards should look on complaisantly while English traders from China—Meares and Hanna and Barkley and Douglas—were taking possession of Nootka. The answer came unexpectedly. Just as the 'Bostonnais' were sailing out for a last run up the coast, there glided into Nootka Sound a proud ship—all sails set, twenty cannon pointed, Spanish colours spread to the breeze. The captain of this vessel, Don Joseph Martinez, took a look at the English fortifications and another at the Americans. The Americans were enemies of England. Therefore the pompous don treated them royally, presented them with spices and wines, and allowed them to depart unmolested. When the Americans returned from the run up coast, they found the English fort dismantled, a Spanish fort erected on Hog Island at the entrance of the sound, and

Douglas's ship—the companion of Meares's vessel—held captive by the Spaniard. Gray and Kendrick now exchanged ships, and sailed for China to dispose of their cargoes of furs and receive in exchange cargoes of tea for Boston. The whole city of Boston welcomed the *Columbia* home in the autumn of 1790. Fifty thousand miles she had ploughed through the seas in three years.

In June 1791 Gray was out again on the *Columbia*. This time he went as far north as the Portland Canal, past the Queen Charlotte Islands, where he met Kendrick on the *Lady Washington*. The quarrel at Nootka between the English and the Spaniards was still going on; so this autumn the two 'Bostonnais' anchored for the winter in Clayoquot Sound—place later to be made famous by tragedy—south of Nootka. Here they built a stockaded fur-post for themselves, which they named Fort Defence. During the winter they built and launched a little coasting schooner, the *Adventure*.

Up at Nootka the Spaniard Gonzales de Haro had replaced Martinez; and his countrymen Quimper and Elisa were daily exploring on the east side of Vancouver Island, where to this day Spanish names tell of their charting. Some of the names, however, were afterwards changed. What is to-day known as Esquimalt, Quimper called Valdes, and Victoria he named Cordoba. Amid much firing of muskets and drinking of wine Quimper took solemn possession of all this territory for Spain. Then, early in August 6 of 1791, he sailed away for Monterey, while Elisa remained at Nootka.

Gray knew that three English vessels which had come from China for furs—Colnett's *Argonaut*, Douglas's *Iphigenia*, and the *Princess Royal*—had been seized by the Spanish at Nootka. Though the fact had not been trumpeted to the world, the Spanish said that their pilots had explored these coasts as early as 1775—at least three years before Cook's landing at Nootka; so that if first exploration counted for possession, Spain had first claim. Whether the Spaniards instigated the raid that now threatened the rival American fort at Clayoquot, the two 'Bostonnais' never knew. The *Columbia* had been beached and dismantled. Loop-holes punctured the palisades of the fort, and cannon were above the gates. Sentinels kept constant guard; but what was Gray's horror to learn in February 1792 that Indians to the number of two thousand were in ambush round the fort and had bribed a Hawaiian boy to wet the priming of the 'Bostonnais' guns. The fort could not be defended against such a number of enemies, for there were not twenty men within the walls. Gray hastily got the *Columbia* ready for sea. Having stowed in the hold enough provisions to carry them home if flight should become necessary, the sailors worked in the dark to their necks in water scraping the hull free of barnacles, and when the high tide came in, she was floated out with all on board. On the morning of the 20th the woods were seen to be alive with Indians. The Indians had not counted on their prey escaping by sea, and an old chief came suavely aboard offering Gray sea-otter skins if the 'Bostonnais' would go ashore to trade. Gray slapped the old rascal across the face; the Indian was over the side at a plunge, and the marauders were seen no more.

In spite of the difficulties and dangers it presented, Gray determined to make another effort to find the river which old Bruno Heceta had sighted in 1775. And early in April, after sending his mate north on the little vessel *Adventure* to trade, Gray sailed away south on the *Columbia*. Let us leave him for the present stealing furtively along the coast from Cape Flattery to Cape Disappointment.

----~~~----

It was the spring of 1792. The Spaniard Elisa of Nootka had for a year kept his pilot Narvaez, in a crazy little schooner crowded with thirty sailors, charting north-east past the harbour of Victoria, through Haro Strait, following very much the same channel that steamers follow to-day as they ply between Victoria and Vancouver. East of a high island, where holiday folk now have their summer camps. Pilot Narvaez came on the estuary of a great river, which he called Boca de

Callicum and Maquinna, Chiefs of the Nootka Sound.
FROM MEARES'S *VOYAGES*

Florida Blanca. This could not be Bruno Heceta's river, for this was farther north and inland. It was a new river, with wonderful purple water—the purple of river silt blending with ocean blue. The banks were wooded to the very water's edge with huge-girthed and mossed trees, such as we to-day see in Stanley Park, Vancouver. The river swept down behind a deep harbour, with forested heights between river-mouth and roadstead, as if nature had purposely interposed to guard this harbour against the deposit of silt borne down by the mighty stream. To-day a boulevard rises from the land-locked harbour and goes over the heights to the river-mouth like the arc of a bow; the finest residences of the Canadian Pacific coast stand there; and the river is lined with mile upon mile of lumberyards and saw-mills. Where the rock projects like a hand into the turbid waters stands a crowded city, built like New York on what is almost an island. Where the opposite shores slope down in a natural park are rising the buildings of a great university. The ragged starveling crew of Pilot Narvaez had found what are now known as Burrard Inlet, Vancouver City, Point Grey, Shaughnessy Heights, and the Fraser River. The crew were presently all ill of scurvy, possibly because of the unsanitary crowding, and the schooner, almost falling to pieces, came crawling back to Nootka. The poor Mexicans were utterly unaware that they had discovered a gateway for northern empire. Narvaez himself lay almost unconscious in his berth. Elisa sent them all home to Mexico on furlough; and, on hearing their report, the viceroy of Mexico ordered out two ships, the *Sutil* and the *Mexicana*, Don Galiano and Don Valdes in command, to follow up the charting of the coast northward from Vancouver Island to the Russian settlements.

Small ringing of bells, no blaring of trumpets at all, prayers a-plenty, but little ammunition and less food, accompanied the deep-sea voyagings of these poor Spanish pilots. When Bering set out, he had the power of the whole Russian empire behind him. When Cook set out, he had the power of the whole British Navy behind him. But when the poor Mexican peons set out, they had nothing behind them but the branding iron, or slavery in the mines, if they failed. Yet they sang as they sailed their rickety death-traps, and they laughed as they rowed; and when the tide-rip caught them, they sank without a cry to any but the Virgin. Look at a map of the west coast of the Pacific from the Horn to Sitka. First were the Spaniards at every harbour gate; and yet to-day, of all their deep-sea findings on that coast, not a rod, not a foot, does Spain own. It was, of course, Spain's insane policy of keeping the Pacific 'a closed sea' that concealed the achievements of the Mexican pilots and buried them in oblivion. But if actual accomplishments count, these pilots with their ragged peon crews, half-bloods of Aztec woman and Spanish adventurer, deserve higher rank in the roll of Pacific coast exploration than history has yet accorded them.

England, it may be believed, did not calmly submit to seeing the ships and forts of her traders seized at Nootka. It was not that England cared for the value of three vessels engaged in foreign trade. Still less did she care for the log-huts dignified by the name of a fort. But she was mistress of the seas, and had been since the destruction of the Armada. And as mistress of the seas, she could not tolerate as much as the seizure of a fishing-smack. For some time there were mutterings of war, but at length diplomacy prevailed. England demanded, among other things, the restoration of the buildings and the land, and full reparation for all losses. Spain decided to submit, and accordingly the Nootka Convention was signed by the two powers in October 1790. Two ships, the *Discovery* and the *Chatham*, were then fitted out by the British Admiralty for an expedition to the Pacific to receive formal surrender of the property from Spain, and also to chart the whole coast of the Pacific from Drake's New Albion to the Russian possessions at Sitka. This expedition was commanded by Captain George Vancouver, who had been on the Pacific with Cook. It was April 1792 when Vancouver came up abreast of Cape Disappointment. Was it chance, or fate, that a gale drove him off-shore just two weeks before a rival explorer entered the mouth of the great unknown river that lay on his vessel's starboard bow? But for this mishap Vancouver might have discovered the Columbia, and England might have made good her claim to the territory which is now Oregon and Washington and Idaho. Vancouver's ships were gliding into the Strait of Juan de Fuca when they met a square-hulled, trim little trader under the flag of the United States. It was the *Columbia*, commanded by Robert Gray. The American told an astounding story. He had found Bruno Heceta's River of the West. Vancouver refused to credit the news; yet there was the ship's log; there were the details—landmarks, soundings, anchorages for twenty miles up the Columbia from its mouth. Gray had, indeed, been up the river, and had crossed the bar and come out on the Pacific again.

Vancouver now headed his ships inland and proceeded to explore Puget Sound. Never before had white men's boats cruised the waters of that spider-shaped sea. Every inlet of the tortuous coasts was penetrated and surveyed, to make certain that no passage to the north-east lay through these waters. In June the explorers passed up the Strait of Georgia. A thick fog hid from them what would have proved an important discovery—the mouth of the Fraser river. Some distance north of Burrard Inlet the explorers met the two Spanish ships which the viceroy of Mexico had sent out, the *Sutil* and the *Mexicana*, commanded respectively by Don Galiano and Don Valdes. From them Vancouver learned that Don Quadra, the Spanish representative, was awaiting him at Nootka, prepared to restore the forts and property as agreed in the Nootka Convention. The vessels continued their journey northward and entered Queen Charlotte Sound in August. Then, steering into the open sea, Vancouver sailed for Nootka to meet Spain's official messenger. He had circumnavigated Vancouver Island.

The Nootka controversy had almost caused a European war. Now it ended in what has a resemblance to a comic opera. Vancouver found the Spaniards occupying a fort on an island at the mouth of the harbour. On the main shore stood the Indian village of Chief Maquinna. A Spanish pilot guided the English ship to mooring. The Spanish frigates fairly bristled with cannon. An English officer dressed in regimentals marched to the Spanish fort and presented Captain Vancouver's compliments to Don Quadra. Spanish cannon thundered a welcome that shook the hills, and English guns made answer. A curious fashion, to waste good powder without taking aim at each other, thought Chief Maquinna. Don Quadra breakfasted Captain Vancouver. Captain Vancouver wined and dined Don Quadra; and Maquinna, lord of the wilds, attended the feast dressed Indian fashion. But when the Spanish don and the English officer took breath from flow of compliments and wine, they did not seem to arrive anywhere in their negotiations. Vancouver held that Spain must relinquish the site of Meares's fort and the territory surrounding it and Port Cox. Don Quadra held that he had been instructed to relinquish only the land on which the fort stood—according to Vancouver, 'but little more than one hundred yards in extent any way.' No understanding could be arrived at, and Quadra at the end of September took his departure for Monterey, leaving Vancouver to follow a few days later.

Vancouver was anxious to be off on further exploration. He was eager to verify the existence of the river which Gray had reported. He spent most of October exploring this river. Explorers in that day, as in this, were not fair judges of each other's feats. Vancouver took possession of the Columbia river region for England, setting down in his narrative that 'no other civilized nation or state had ever entered this river before . . . it does not appear that Mr Gray either saw or was ever within five leagues of the entrance.'

Vancouver then visited the presidio at San Francisco, and thence proceeded to Monterey, where Quadra awaited him. His lieutenant,

George Vancouver.

Broughton, who had been in charge of the boats that explored the Columbia, here left him and accompanied Quadra to San Blas, whence he went overland to the Atlantic and sailed for England, bearing dispatches to the government. Vancouver spent yet another year on the North Pacific, corroborating his first year's charting and proving that no north-east passage through the continent existed. Portland Canal, Jervis Inlet, Cook Inlet, Prince William Sound, Lynn Canal—all were traced to head-waters by Vancouver.

The curtain then drops on the exploration of the North Pacific, with Spain jealously holding all south of the Columbia, Russia jealously holding all north of Sitka, and England and the United States advancing counter-claims for all the territory between.

'ALEXANDER MACKENZIE, FROM CANADA, BY LAND'

The movement of the fur traders towards the Pacific now became a fevered race for the wealth of a new El Dorado. Astor's traders in New York, the Scottish and English merchants of the North-West Company in Montreal, the Spanish traders of the South-West, even the directors of the sleepy old Hudson's Bay Company—all turned longing eyes to that Pacific north-west coast whence came sea-otter skins in trade, each for a few pennies' worth of beads, powder, or old iron. Rumours, too, were rife of the great wealth of the seal rookeries, and the seal proved as powerful a magnet to draw the fur traders as the little beaver, the pursuit of which had led them into frozen wilds.

Up in the Athabaska country, eating his heart out with chagrin because his associates in the North-West Company of Montreal had ignored his voyage of discovery down the Mackenzie river to the Arctic in 1789,[1] the young trader Alexander Mackenzie heard these rumours of new wealth in furs on the Pacific. Who would be the first overland to that western sea? If Spaniard and Russian had tapped the source of wealth from the ocean side, why could not the Nor'westers cross the mountains and secure the furs from the land side? Mackenzie had heard, too, of the fabled great River of the West. Could he but catch the swish of its upper current, what would hinder him floating down it to the sea? Mackenzie thought and thought, and paced his quarters up at Fort Chipewyan, on Lake Athabaska, till his mind became so filled with the idea of an overland journey to the Pacific that he could not sleep or rest. He had felt himself handicapped by lack of knowledge of astronomy and surveying when on the voyage to the Arctic, so he asked leave of absence from his company, came down by canoe to Montreal, and sailed for England to spend the winter studying in London. Here, everything was in a ferment over the voyages of Cook and Hanna and Meares, over the seizure of British trading-ships by the viceroy of Mexico, over the Admiralty's plans to send Vancouver out to complete Cook's explorations. The rumours were as fuel to the flame that burned in Mackenzie. The spring of 1792 saw him hurrying back to Fort Chipewyan to prepare for the expedition on which he had set his heart. When October came he launched his canoes, fully manned and provisioned, on Lake Athabaska, and, ascending the Peace river to a point about six miles above the forks formed by its junction with the Smoky, he built a rude palisaded fur-post and spent the winter there.

Spring came and found Mackenzie ready to go forward into the unknown regions of the west, regions as yet untrodden by the feet of white men. Alexander Mackay, one of the most resolute and capable traders in the service of the North-West Company, was to be his companion on the journey; and with them were to go six picked French-Canadian voyageurs and two Indians as guides. They had built a birch-bark canoe of exceptional strength and lightness. It was twenty-five feet long, some four feet in beam, twenty-six inches deep, and had a carrying capacity of three thousand pounds. Explorers and canoe-men stepped into their light craft on the evening of May 9, 1793. The fort fired guns and waved farewell; the paddlers struck up a voyageurs' song; and the blades dipped in rhythmic time. Mackenzie waved his hat back to the group in front of the fort gate; and then with set face headed his canoe west-ward for the Pacific.

Recall what was happening now out on the Pacific! Robert Gray was heading home to Boston with news of the discovery of the great river. Vancouver was back from San Francisco carefully charting the inner channel of the coast. Baranoff, the little czar of the Russian traders, was coasting at the head of fifteen hundred 'bidarkies' between the Aleutians and Sitka; and Spain was still sending out ragged pilots to chart the seas which she had not the marine to hold.

The big canoe went on, up the Peace river. Spring thaw brought the waters down from the mountains in turbulent floods, and the precipices narrowed on each side till the current became a foaming cascade. It was one thing to float down-stream with brigades of singing voyageurs and cargoes of furs in spring; it was a different matter to breast the full force of these torrents with only ten men to paddle. In the big brigades the men paddled in relays. In this canoe each man was expected to pole and paddle continuously and fiercely against a current that was like a mill-race. Mackenzie listened to the grumblers over the night camp-fire, and explained how much safer it was to ascend an unknown stream with bad rapids than to run down it. The danger could always be seen before running into it. He cheered the drooping spirits of his band, and inspired them with some of his own indomitable courage.

By May 16 the river had narrowed to a foaming cataract; and the banks were such sheer rock-wall that it was almost impossible to land. They had arrived at the Rocky Mountain Portage, as it was afterwards called. It was clear that the current could not be stemmed by pole or paddle; the canoe must be towed or carried. When Mackenzie tried to get foothold or handhold on the shore, huge boulders and land-slides of loose earth slithered down, threatening to smash canoe and canoemen. Mackenzie got out a tow-line eighty feet long. This he tied to the port thwart of the canoe. With the tow-line round his shoulders, while the torrent roared past and filled the canyon with the 'voice of many waters,' Mackenzie leaped to the dangerous slope, cut foothold and handhold on the face of the cliff with an axe, and scrambled up to a table of level rock. Then he shouted and signalled for his men to come up. If the voyageurs had not been hemmed in by a boiling maelstrom on both sides, they would have deserted on the spot. Mackenzie saw them begin to strip as if to swim; then, clothes on back and barefoot, they scrambled up the treacherous shore. He reached over, and assisted them to the level ground above. The tow-line was drawn taut round trees and the canoe tracked up the raging current. But the rapids became wilder. A great wave struck the bow of the canoe and the tow-line snapped in mid-air. The terrified men looking over the edge of the precipice saw their craft sidle as if to swamp; but, on the instant, another mighty wave flung her ashore, and they were able to haul her out of danger.

Mackay went ahead to see how far the rapids extended. He found that they were at least nine miles in length. On his return the men were declaring that they would not ascend such waters another rod. Mackenzie, to humour them, left them to a regale of rum and pemmican, and axe in hand went up the precipitous slope, and began to make a rough path through the forest. Up the rude incline the men hauled the empty canoe, cutting their way as they advanced. Then they carried up the provisions in ninety-pound bundles. By nightfall of the first day they had advanced but one mile. Next morning the journey was continued; the progress was exactly three miles the second day, and the men fell in their tracks with exhaustion, and slept that night where they lay. But at length they had passed the rapids; the toilsome portage was over, and the canoe was again launched on the stream. The air was icy from the snows of the mountain-peaks, and in spite of their severe exercise the men had to wear heavy clothing.

On May 31 they arrived at the confluence where the rivers now known as the Finlay and the Parsnip, flowing together, form the Peace. The Indians of this region told Mackenzie of a great river beyond the big mountains, a river that flowed towards the noonday sun; and of 'Carrier Indians'² inland, who acted as middlemen and traders between the coast and the mountain tribes. They said that the Carriers told legends of 'white men on the coast, who wore armour from head to heel'—undoubtedly the Spanish dons—and of 'huge canoes with sails like clouds' that plied up and down 'the stinking waters'—meaning the sea.

Mackenzie was uncertain which of the two confluents to follow—whether to ascend the Finlay, flowing from the north-west, or the Parsnip, flowing from the south-east. He consulted his Indian guides, one of whom advised him to take the southern branch. This would lead, the guide said, to a lake from which they could portage to another stream, and so reach the great river leading to the sea. Mackenzie decided to follow this advice, and ordered his men to proceed up the Parsnip. Their hearts sank. They had toiled up one terrible river; directly before them was another, equally precipitous and dangerous. Nevertheless, they began the ascent. For a week the rush of avalanches from the mountain-peaks could be heard like artillery fire. Far up above the cloud-line they could see the snow tumbling over an upper precipice in powdery wind-blown cataracts; a minute later would come the thunderous rumble of the falling masses. With heroic fortitude the voyageurs held their way against the fierce current, sometimes paddling, sometimes towing the canoe along the river-bank. Once, however, when Mackenzie and Mackay had gone ahead on foot to reconnoitre, ordering the canoemen to paddle along behind, the canoe failed to follow. Mackay went back and found the voyageurs disputing ashore. They pretended that a leak had delayed them. From Indians met by the way, Mackenzie learned that he was indeed approaching a portage over the height-of-land to the waters that flowed towards the Pacific. One of these Indians was induced to go with Mackenzie as guide. They tramped ahead through a thicket of brush, and came suddenly out on a blue tarn. This was the source of the Parsnip, the southern branch of the Peace. The whole party arrived on June 12. A portage of 817 paces over a rocky ridge brought them to a second mountain lake drained by a river that flowed towards the west. Mackenzie had crossed the watershed, the Great Divide, and had reached the waters which empty into the Pacific.

The river which the explorers now entered was a small tributary of the Fraser. Some years later it was named by Simon Fraser the Bad River, and it deserved the name. Mackenzie launched his canoe down-stream. The men's spirits rose. This was working with the current, not against it; but the danger of going with an unknown current became at once apparent. The banks began to skim past, the waters to rise in oily corrugations; and before the voyageurs realized it, they were caught by a current they could not stem and were hurried sidling down-stream. The men sprang out to swim, but the current prevented them from reaching land, and they clung in terror to the sides of the canoe till an eddy sent them on a sand-bar in the midst of the rapids. With great difficulty the craft was rescued and brought ashore. The stem had been torn out of the canoe, half the powder and bullets lost, and the entire cargo drenched.

The men were panic-stricken and on the verge of mutiny; but Mackenzie was undaunted and determined to go forward. He spread the provisions out to dry and set his crew to work patching up the stern of the broken canoe with resin and oilcloth and new cedar lining. That night the mountain Indian who had acted as guide across the portage gave Mackenzie the slip and escaped in the woods. For several days after this most of the party trudged on foot carrying the cargo, while four of the most experienced canoemen brought the empty canoe down the rapids. But on June 17 they found further progress by water impossible owing to masses of driftwood in the stream. They were now, however, less than a mile from the south fork of the Fraser; the men carried the canoe on their shoulders across the intervening neck of swamp, and at last the explorers 'enjoyed the inexpressible satisfaction' of finding themselves on the banks of a broad, navigable river, on the west side of the Great Divide.

The point where they embarked, on the morning of June 18, was about thirty-five miles above the Nechaco, or north fork of the Fraser, just at the upper end of the great bend where the south fork, flowing to the north-west, sweeps round in a semicircle, joins its confluent, and pours southward to the sea. This trend of the river to the south was not what Mackenzie expected. He wanted to follow a stream leading west. Without noticing it, he had passed the north fork, the Nechaco, and was sweeping down the main stream of the Fraser, where towering mountains cut off the view ahead, and the powerful rush of the waters foreboded hard going, if not more rapids and cataracts. Mackenzie must have a new guide. The Carrier Indians dwelt along this river, but they appeared to be truculently hostile. On June 21 a party of these Indians stood on one of the banks and shot arrows at the explorers and rolled stones from the precipices. Mackenzie landed on the opposite bank, after sending a hunter by a wide detour through the woods behind the Indians on the other shore, with orders to shoot instantly if the savages threatened either the canoe or himself. In full sight of the Indians Mackenzie threw trinkets in profusion on the ground, laid down his musket and pistol, and held up his arms in token of friendship. The savages understood the meaning of his actions. Two of them jumped into a dug-out and came poling across to him. Suspiciously and very timidly they landed. Mackenzie threw himself on the ground, and on the sands traced his path through the 'shining mountains.' By Indian sign-language he told them he wanted to go to the sea; and, disarmed of all suspicion, the Indians were presently on the ground beside him, drawing the trail to the sea. Terrible rapids (they imitated the noise of the cataracts) barred his way by this river. He must turn back to where another river (the Blackwater) came in on the west, and ascend that stream to a portage which would lead over to the sea.

The post of Alexandria on the Cariboo Road marks Mackenzie's farthest south on the Fraser. At this point, after learning all he could of the route from the Indians, he turned the prow of his canoe up the river. The Carrier Indians provided him with a guide. On July 4, nearly two months from the time of leaving the fort on the Peace river, the portage on the Blackwater was reached; the canoe was abandoned, some provisions were cached, and each man set off afoot with a ninety-pound pack on his back. Heavy mist lay on the thick forest. The Indian trail was but a dimly defined track over forest mould. The dripping underbrush that skirted the path soaked the men to the skin. The guide had shown an inclination to desert, and Mackenzie slept beside him, ready to seize and hold him on the slightest movement. Totem cedar-poles in front of the Indian villages told the explorers that they were approaching the home of the coastal tribes. The men's clothing was by this time torn to shreds. They were barefooted, bareheaded, almost naked. For nearly two weeks they journeyed on foot; then, having forded the Dean river, they embarked for the sea on the Bella Coola in cedar dug-outs which they procured from Indians of one of the coastal tribes. Daily now Mackenzie saw signs of white traders. The Indians possessed beads and trinkets. One Indian had a Spanish or Russian lance. Fishing weirs were passed. There was a whiff of salt water in the air; then far out between the hills lay a gap of illimitable blue. At eight o'clock in the morning of Saturday, July 20, 1793, Mackenzie reached the mouth of the river and found himself on the sea. The next day he went down North Bentinck Arm, and, passing the entrance to the south arm, landed at the cape on the opposite shore. He then proceeded down Burke Channel. It was near the mouth of this inlet that he inscribed, in red letters on a large rock, the memorable words: '*Alexander Mackenzie, from Canada, by land, the twenty-second of July, one thousand seven hundred and ninety-three. Lat. 52° 20' 48' N.*'

Barely two months previously Vancouver had explored and named these very waters and headlands. A hostile old Indian explained bellicosely that the white sailors had fired upon him. For this outrage he demanded satisfaction in gifts from Mackenzie. Few gifts had Mackenzie for the aggressive old chief. There were exactly twenty pounds of pemmican—two pounds a man for a three months' trip back. There remained also fifteen pounds of rice—the mainstay of the voyageurs—and six pounds of mouldy flour. The Indians proved so vociferously hostile that two voyageurs had to stand guard while the others slept on the bare rocks. On one occasion savages in dug-outs began hurling spears. But no harm resulted from these unfriendly demonstrations, and the party of explorers presently set out on their homeward journey.

Mackenzie had accomplished his object. In the race to the Pacific overland he was the first of the explorers of North America to cross the continent and reach the ocean. Late in August the voyageurs were back at the little fort on the Peace river. Mackenzie shortly afterwards quitted the fur country and retired to Scotland, where he wrote the story of his explorations. His book appeared in 1801, and in the following year he was knighted by the king for his great achievements.

THE DESCENT OF THE FRASER RIVER

Amerifcan traders were not slow to follow up the discovery of Robert Gray on the Pacific. Spain, the pioneer pathfinder, had ceded Louisiana to France; and France, by way of checkmating British advance in North America, had sold Louisiana to the United States for fifteen million dollars. What did Louisiana include? Certainly, from New Orleans to the Missouri. Did it also include from the Missouri to Gray's river, the Columbia? The United States had sent Meriwether Lewis and William Clark overland from the Missouri to the Columbia, ostensibly on a scientific expedition, but in reality to lay claim to the new territory for the United States. This brings the exploration of the Pacific down to 1806.

Take a look at the map! Mackenzie had crossed overland from the Peace river to Bella Coola. Who was to own the great belt of empire—a third larger than Germany—between Mackenzie's trail westward and Lewis and Clark's trail to the mouth of the Columbia? In 1805 Simon Fraser, who as a child had come from the United States to Canada with his widowed mother in the Loyalist migration, and now in his thirtieth year was a partner in the North-West Company of Montreal, had crossed the Rockies by way of the Peace river. He had followed Mackenzie's trail over the terrible nine-mile carrying-place and had built there a fur-post—Rocky Mountain Portage. He had ascended that same Parsnip river, which Mackenzie had found so appalling, to a little emerald lake set like a jewel in the mountains. There he had built another fur-trading post, and named it after his friend, Archibald Norman McLeod. This was the first fur-post known to have been erected in the interior of New Caledonia, now British Columbia. The new fort had been left in charge of James McDougall; and during the winter of 1806 McDougall had crossed the heavily drifted carrying-place and descended the Bad River as far as the south fork of the Fraser, which all traders at that time mistook for the upper reaches of Gray's Columbia. Instead of going down the main stream of the Fraser, McDougall ascended both the Nechaco and the Stuart; and if he did not actually behold the beautiful alpine tarns since known as Fraser Lake and Stuart Lake, he was at least the first white man to hear of them.

In May of 1806, after sending the year's furs from Rocky Mountain Portage east to Fort Chipewyan, Simon Fraser set out to explore this inland empire concerning which McDougall had reported. John Stuart accompanied Fraser as lieutenant. They crossed from the head-waters of the Parsnip to the south fork of the Fraser, and on June 10 camped at the mouth of the Nechaco. Towards the end of July the Carriers camped on Stuart Lake were amazed to see advancing across the waters, with rhythmic gallop of paddles, two enormous birch canoes. When the canoes reached the land Fraser and Stuart stepped ashore, and a volley was fired to celebrate the formal taking possession of a new inland empire. What to do with the white men's offerings of tobacco the Carriers did not know. They thought the white men in smoking were emitting spirits with each breath. When the traders offered soap to the squaws, the women at once began to devour it. The result was a frothing at the mouth as amazing to them as the smoke from the men. History does not record whether the women became as addicted to soap as the men to the fragrant weed.

Active trading with the Indians began at once. The lake was named Stuart in honour of Fraser's companion, and the ground was cleared for a palisaded fort, which, when erected, they named Fort St. James. The scene was enchanting. The lake wound for a distance of fifty miles amid the foot-hills of the mighty forested mountains. It was four or five miles wide, and was gemmed with green islets; and all round, appearing through the clouds in jagged outline, were the opal summits of the snowy peaks. No wonder the two Scotsmen named the new inland empire New Caledonia—after their native land.

It will be remembered that McDougall had heard of another mountain tarn. This was forty miles south of Stuart Lake, at the head-waters of the Nechaco, the north fork of the Fraser. Stuart went overland south to spy out the southern lake; and his report was of such an entrancing region—heavily forested, with an abundance of game and fish—that Fraser glided down the Stuart river and poled up the Nechaco to the lake which Stuart had already named after his chief. Again a fort was erected and named Fort Fraser, making three forts in the interior of New Caledonia.

Fraser had sent a request to the directors of the North-West Company to be permitted to fit out an expedition down the great river, which he thought was the Columbia; and in the spring of 1807 two canoes under Jules Quesnel were sent out with goods. Quesnel arrived at Fort St. James in the autumn, bringing from the east the alarming word that Lewis and Clark had gone overland and taken possession of all the territory between the Missouri and the mouth of the Columbia. No time was to be lost by Fraser in establishing a claim to the region to the west of the Rockies between the Peace and the Columbia. Fraser went down the river and strengthened British possession by building a fourth fort—Fort George at the mouth of the Nechaco. This was to be the starting-point of the expedition to the Pacific. Then, towards the end of May 1808, he set out down the great river with four canoes, nineteen voyageurs, and Stuart and Quesnel as first assistants.

Fifteen miles below the fort the river walls narrowed and the canoes swept into the roaring cataract of Fort George canyon. The next day they shot through the Cottonwood canyon, and paused at the point thenceforth to be known as Quesnel. On the third day they passed Mackenzie's farthest south—the site of the present Alexandria. Below this the river was unexplored and unknown. Suddenly the enormous flood-waters swollen by melting mountain snows contracted to a width of only forty yards, and with a fearful roar swept into a rock-walled gorge. In sublime unconsciousness of heroism Fraser records:

> As it was impossible to carry the canoes across the land owing to the height of the steep hills, we resolved to venture down. I ordered the five best men of the crews into a canoe lightly loaded; and in a moment it was under way. After passing the first cascade she lost her head and was drawn into an eddy, where she was whirled about, in suspense whether to sink or swim. However, she took a turn from this vortex, flying from one danger to another; but, in spite of every effort, the whirlpool forced her against a low rock. Upon this the men scrambled out, saving their lives; but the greatest difficulty was still ahead. To continue by water would be certain destruction. During this distressing scene we were on shore looking on; but the situation rendered our approach perilous. The bank was high and steep. We had to plunge our daggers into the ground to avoid sliding into the river. We cut steps, fastened a line to the front of the canoe, and hauled it up. Our lives hung upon a thread, as one false step might have hurled us into eternity. However, we cleared the bank before dark. The men had to ascend the immense hills with heavy loads on their backs.

Indians warned the white men to desist from their undertaking. Better, they advised, go overland eastward to a great peaceful river and descend that to the sea. Fraser, of course, did not know that the peaceful river they spoke of was really the Columbia. He thought the river he was following was the Columbia. With the help of Indians the canoes were pulled up-hill, and horses were hired from them to carry the provisions overland. Below this portage, as they continued the descent, an enormous crag spread across the river, appearing at first to bar the passage ahead. This was Bar Rock. Beyond it several minor rapids were passed without difficulty; and then they came upon a series of great whirlpools which seemed impassable. But the men unloaded the canoes and—'a desperate undertaking'—ran them down the rapids with light ballast. They then came back overland for the packs.

> This task [says Fraser] was as dangerous as going by water. The men passed and repassed a declivity, on loose stones and gravel, which constantly gave way under foot. One man, who lost the path, got in a most intricate and perilous position. With a large package on his back, he got so wedged amid the rocks that he could move neither forward nor backward, nor yet unload himself. I crawled, not without great risk, to his assistance, and saved his life by cutting his pack so [that] it dropped back in the river. On this carrying-place, which was two miles long, our shoes became shattered.

For several days after this the advance was by a succession of rapids and portages. On June 9 the stream again narrowed to forty yards and swept violently between two overhanging precipices.

> The water, which rolls down this passage in tumultuous waves and with great velocity, had a frightful appearance. However, it being absolutely impossible to carry canoes by land, all hands without hesitation embarked on the mercy of the awful tide. Once on the water, the die was cast; and the

difficulty consisted in keeping the canoes clear of the precipice on one side and clear of the gulfs formed by the waves
on the other. Thus skimming along as fast as lightning, the
crews, cool and determined, followed each other in awful
silence; and when we arrived at the end, we stood gazing
at each other in silent congratulation on our narrow escape
from total destruction. After breathing a little, we continued our course to the point where the Indians camped.

The natives here warned Fraser that it would be madness to go
forward. At the same time they furnished him with a guide. The
same evening the party reached the place described by Fraser as 'a
continual series of cascades cut by rocks and bounded by precipices
that seemed to have no end.' Never had he seen 'anything so dreary
and dangerous.' Towering above were 'mountains upon mountains
whose summits are covered with eternal snow.' An examination
of the river for some distance below convinced Fraser that it was
impossible of navigation, and he decided to make the remainder of
the journey on foot. After building a scaffold, on which the canoes
and some provisions were placed and covered with underbrush and
moss, the party, on June 11, began their tramp down the river-bank.
Each man carried on his back a ninety-pound pack, supported by
a strap across the forehead. Again and again on the journey Indians
confronted Fraser with hostile show of weapons, but the intrepid
trader disarmed hostility by gifts. The Indians declared that the
sea lay only ten 'sleeps' distant. One of the chiefs said that he had
himself seen white men, who were great 'tyees,' because 'they were
well dressed and very proud and went about this way'—clipping his
hands to his hips and strutting about with an air of vast importance.
The Indians told Fraser of another great river that came in from
the east and joined this one some distance below. He had passed
the site of the present Lillooet and was approaching the confluence
of the Thompson with the Fraser. Farther down European articles

Simon Fraser.

AFTER THE PORTRAIT IN THE PARLIAMENT BUILDINGS, VICTORIA, BC

were seen among the Indians. It was the fishing season, and the tribes had assembled in great hordes. Here the river was navigable, and three wooden dug-outs were obtained from the natives for the descent to the sea. The voyageurs again embarked, and swept down the narrow bends of the turbulent floods at what are now Lytton, Yale, and Hope. There were passes where the river was such a raging torrent that the dug-outs had to be carried overland. There were places where Fraser's voyageurs had to climb precipices by means of frail ladders, made of poles and withes, that swayed to their tread and threatened to precipitate them into the torrent beneath.

When the river turned sharply west, Fraser could not help noticing that the Indians became more violently hostile. Far south could be seen the opal dome of Mount Baker, named by Vancouver after one of his lieutenants. As they advanced, the banks lowered to reedy swamps and mosquitoes appeared in clouds. What troubled Fraser most was the fact that the river lay many miles north of the known latitude of the Columbia. It daily grew on him that this could not possibly be the Columbia. The tide rose and fell in the river. The Indian guide begged the white men not to go on; he was afraid, he said, of the Indians of the sea-coast. The river channel divided. Natives along the shore began singing war-songs and beating the war-drum; then they circled out threateningly round the white men's boats. Signs were seen of the sea ahead; but the Indians were 'howling like wolves and brandishing war-clubs,' and Fraser concluded that it would be unwise to delay longer amid such dangers. To his intense disappointment he had established the latitude as 49°, whereas the Columbia was in latitude 46° 20'. 'This river is therefore *not* the Columbia,' he declared. 'If I had been convinced of this when I left my canoes, I would certainly have returned.'

The return journey was fraught with danger. Always one man stood guard while the others slept; and again and again the little party was surrounded by ferociously hostile bands. Between apprehension of the dangers of the wild trail of the Fraser canyons and fear of hostile natives, the men became so panic-stricken that they threw down their paddles and declared their intention of trying to escape overland through the mountains. Fraser reasoned and remonstrated, and finally threatened. After so much heroism he would not permit cowardly desertion. Then he forced each voyageur to swear on the Cross: 'I do solemnly swear that I will sooner perish than forsake in distress any of our crew during the present voyage.' With renewed self-respect they then paddled off, singing voyageurs' songs to keep up their courage. Imagine, for a moment, the scene! The turbid, mad waters of the Fraser hemmed in between rock walls, carving a living way through the adamant; banks from which red savages threw down rocks wherever the wild current drove the dugout inshore; and, tossed by the waves—a chip-like craft containing nineteen ragged men singing like schoolboys! Once away from the coastal tribes, however, the white men were aided by the inland Carriers. They found the canoes and supplies in perfect condition and unmolested, though hundreds of Carrier Indians must have passed where lay the belongings of the white strangers. On August 5, to the inexpressible relief of Fort George, the little band once more were at their headquarters in New Caledonia.

THOMPSON AND THE ASTORIANS

While Fraser was working down the wild canyons of the great river which now bears his name, other fur traders were looking towards the Pacific ocean. In 1810 John Jacob Astor, a New York merchant, who bought furs from the Nor'westers in Montreal for shipment to Germany, formed the Pacific Fur Company, and took into its service a number of the partners and servants of the North-West Company. Some of these men were dispatched round the Horn in the *Tonquin* to the mouth of the Columbia; while another party went overland from Mackinaw and St. Louis, following the trail of Lewis and Clark. One of the Nor'westers who entered Astor's service was Alexander Mackay, Mackenzie's companion on the journey to the coast; another was a brother of the Stuart who had accompanied Fraser through New Caledonia; and a third was a brother of the McDougall who commanded Fort McLeod, the first fort built by the Nor'westers in New Caledonia.

In the light of subsequent developments, it is a matter for speculation whether these Nor'westers joined Astor purposely to overthrow his scheme in the interests of their old company; or were later bribed to desert him; or, as is most likely, simply grew dissatisfied with the inexperienced, blundering mismanagement of Astor's company, and reverted gladly to their old service. However that may have been, it is certain that the North-West Company did not fail to take notice of the plans that Astor had set afoot for the Pacific fur trade; for in a secret session of the partners, at Fort William on Lake Superior, '*it was decided in council that the Company should send to Columbia River, where the Americans had established Astoria, and that a party should proceed overland to the coast.*'

It puzzled the Nor'westers to learn that the river Fraser had explored in 1808 was not the Columbia. Where, then, were the upper reaches of the great River of the West which Gray and Vancouver had reported? The company issued urgent instructions to its traders in the Far West to keep pushing up the North and South Saskatchewan, up the Red Deer, up the Bow, up the Athabaska, up the Smoky, up the Pembina, and to press over the mountains wherever any river led oceanwards through the passes. This duty of finding new passable ways to the sea was especially incumbent on the company's surveyor and astronomer, David Thompson. He was formerly of the Hudson's Bay Company, but had come over to the Nor'westers, and in their service had surveyed from the Assiniboine to the Missouri and from Lake Superior to the Saskatchewan.

Towards the spring of 1799 Thompson had been on the North Saskatchewan and had moved round the region of Lesser Slave Lake. That year, at Grand Portage, at the annual meeting of the traders of the North-West Company, he was ordered to begin a thorough exploration of the mountains; and the spring of 1800 saw him at Rocky Mountain House[1] on the upper reaches of the North Saskatchewan above the junction of the Clearwater. Hitherto the Nor'westers had crossed the mountains by way of the Peace river. But Thompson was to explore a dozen new trails across the Great Divide. While four of his men crossed over to the Red Deer river and rafted or canoed down the South Saskatchewan, Thompson himself, with five French Canadians and two Indian guides, crossed the mountains to the Kootenay country. The Kootenay Indians were encamped on the Kootenay plains preparatory to their winter's hunt, and Thompson persuaded some of them to accompany him back over the mountains to Rocky Mountain House on the North Saskatchewan. This was the beginning of the trade between the Kootenays and white men. Probably from these Indians Thompson learned of the entrance to the Rockies by the beautiful clear mountain-stream now named the Bow; and Duncan McGillivray, a leading partner, accompanied him south from Rocky Mountain House to the spot on the Bow where to-day the city of Calgary stands. It was on this trip that Nor'westers first met the Piegan Indians. From these horsemen of the plains the explorers learned that it was only a ten-day journey overland to the Missouri. Snow was falling when the traders entered the Rockies at what is now the Gap, on the Canadian Pacific Railway. Inside the gateway to the rugged defile of forest and mountain the traders revelled in the sublime scenery of the Banff valley. At Banff, eastward of Cascade mountain, on the sheltered plain where Kootenays and Stonies used to camp, one can still find the circular mounds that mark a trading-station of this era. Whether the white men discovered the beautiful blue tarn now known as Devil's Lake, or saw the Bow river falls, where tourists to-day fish away long summer afternoons, or dipped in the famous hot springs on the slope of Sulphur mountain, we do not know. They could hardly have met and conversed with the Kootenays and Stonies without hearing about these attractions, which yearly drew Indian families to camp in the encircling moun-tains, while the men ranged afield to hunt.

Thompson and McGillivray were back at Rocky Mountain House on the Saskatchewan for Christmas. Some time during 1800 their French-Canadian voyageurs are known to have crossed Howse Pass, the source of the North Saskatchewan, which was discovered by Duncan McGillivray and named after Joseph Howse of the North-West Company.

For several years after this Thompson was engaged in making surveys for the North-West Company in the valley of the Peace river and between the Saskatchewan and the Churchill. In 1806 we find him in the country south of the Peace, which was then in charge of that Jules Quesnel who was to accompany Fraser in 1808. Fraser, as we have seen, was already busy exploring the region between McLeod Lake and Stuart Lake, and had laid his plans to descend the great river which he thought was Gray's Columbia. Now, while Thompson spent the winter of 1806–7 between the Peace and the North Saskatchewan, trading and exploring, he doubtless learned of Fraser's explorations west of the Rockies and of the vast extent of New Caledonia; and June 1807 saw him over the mountains on the Kootenay plains, where to his infinite delight he came upon a turbulent river, whose swollen current flowed towards the Pacific. 'May God give me to see where its waters flow into the ocean,' he ejaculated. This was, however, but a tributary of the long-sought Columbia. It was the river now called the Blaeberry. Thompson followed down the banks of this stream by a well-known Indian trail, and on June 30 he came to the Columbia itself. Although the river here flowed to the north, he must have known, from the deposits of blue silt and the turgidity of the current, that he had found at least an upper reach of the River of the West; but he could hardly guess that its winding course would lead him a dance of eleven hundred miles before he should reach the sea.

The party camped and built the boats they needed, and a fortnight later they were poling up-stream to the lake we to-day know as Windermere, where Thompson built a fort which he called 'Kootenai.' Here he spent the winter trading, and when the warm Chinook winds cleared away the snows, in April 1808, about the time Fraser was preparing to descend the Fraser river, he paddled up-stream to where the Columbia river has its source in Upper Columbia Lake. A portage of about a mile and a half brought him to another large river, which flowed southward. This stream—the Kootenay—led him south into the country of the Flatheads, then made a great bend and swept to the north. This was disappointing. Thompson returned to his fort on Windermere Lake, packed the furs his men had gathered, and retraced his trail of the previous year to Rocky Mountain House. He had undoubtedly found the River of the West, but he had learned nothing of its course to the sea.

During nearly all of 1809 Thompson was exploring the Kootenay river and its branches through Idaho and Montana. Still no path had he found to the sea. In 1810 he seems to have gone east for instructions from his company. What the instructions were we may conjecture from subsequent developments. Astor of New York, as we have seen, was busy launching his fur traders for operations on the Pacific. Piegan warriors blocked the passage into the Rockies by the North Saskatchewan; so Thompson in the autumn of this year ascended the Athabaska. Winter came early. The passes were filled with snow and beset by warriors. He failed to get provisions down from Rocky Mountain House; and his men, cut off by hostile savages from all help from outside posts, had literally to cut and shovel their way through Athabaska Pass while subsisting on short rations. The men built huts in the pass; some hunted, while others made snow-shoes and sleighs. They were down to rations of dog-meat and moccasins, and hardly knew whether to expect death at the hands of raiding Piegans or from starvation. On New Year's Day of 1811, when the thermometer dropped to 24° below zero, with a biting wind, Thompson was packing four broken-down horses and two dogs over the pass to the west side of the Great Divide. The mountains rose precipitously on each side; but when the trail began dropping down westward, the weather moderated, though the snow grew deeper; and in the third week of January Thompson came on the baffling current of the Columbia. He camped there for the remainder of the winter, near the entrance of the Canoe River. Why he went up the Columbia in the spring, tracing it back to its source, and thence south again into Idaho, instead of rounding the bend and going down the river, we do not know. He was evidently puzzled by the contrary directions in which the great river seemed to flow. At all events, by a route which is not clearly known, Thompson struck the Spokane river in June 1811, near the site of the present city of Spokane; and following down the Spokane, he again found the elusive Columbia and embarked on its waters. At the mouth of the Snake River, on July 9, he erected a pole, on which he hoisted a flag and attached a sheet of paper claiming possession of the country for Great Britain and the North-West Company. A month later, when Astor's traders came up-stream from the mouth of the Columbia, they were amazed to find a British flag 'waving triumphantly' at this spot. Unfortunately, Thompson's claim ignored the fact that both Lewis and Clark and the Astorians had already passed this way on their overland route to the Pacific.

From this point Thompson evidently raced for the Pacific. Within a week he had passed the Dalles, passed the mouth of the Willamette, passed what was to become the site of the Hudson's Bay Company's post of Fort Vancouver; and at midday of Monday, July 15, he swept round a bend of the mighty stream and came within sight of the sea. Crouched between the dank, heavy forests and the heaving river floods, stood a little palisaded and fresh-hewn log fur-post—Astoria. Thompson was two months too late to claim the region of the lower Columbia for the Nor'westers. One can imagine the wild halloo with which the tired voyageurs greeted Astoria when their comrades of old from Athabaska came tumbling hilariously from the fort gates—McDougall of Rocky Mountain House, Stuart of Chipewyan, and John Clarke, whom Thompson had known at Isle à la Crosse. But where was Alexander Mackay, who had gone overland with Mackenzie in 1793? The men fell into one another's arms with gruff, profane embraces. Thompson was haled in to a sumptuous midday dinner of river salmon, duck and partridge, and wines brought round the world. The absence of Mackay was the only thing that took from the pleasure of the occasion.

—m—

A party of the Astorians, as we have seen, had sailed round the Horn on the *Tonquin*; another party had gone overland from Mackinaw and St. Louis. On the *Tonquin* were twenty sailors, four partners, twelve clerks, and thirteen voyageurs. She sailed from New York in September 1810. Jonathan Thorn, the captain, was a retired naval officer, who resented the easy familiarity of the fur traders with their servants, and ridiculed the seasickness of the fresh-water voyageurs. The Tonquin had barely rounded the Horn before the partners and the commander were at sixes and sevens. A landing was made at the mouth of the Columbia in March 1811, and eight lives were lost in an attempt to head small boats up against the tide-rip of river and sea. After endless jangling about where to land, where to build, how to build, the rude fort which Thompson saw had been knocked together. The *Tonquin* sailed up the coast of Vancouver Island to trade. On the vessel went Alexander Mackay to help in the trade with the coastal Indians, whom he was supposed to know. In spite of Mackay's warning that the Nootka tribes were notoriously treacherous and resentful towards white traders, Captain Thorn with lordly indifference permitted them to swarm aboard his vessel. Once when Mackay had gone ashore at Clayoquot, where Gray had wintered twenty years before, Thorn, forgetting that his ship was not a training-school, struck an old chief across the face and threw him over the rail. When Mackay heard what had happened, instead of applauding the captain's valour, he showed the utmost alarm, and begged Thorn to put out for the open sea. The captain smiled in scorn. Twenty Indians were welcomed on the deck the very next day. More came. At the same time the vessel was completely surrounded by a fleet of canoes. As if to throw the white men off all suspicion, the squaws came paddling out, laughing and chatting. Mackay in horror noticed that in the barter all the Indians were taking knives for their furs, and that groups were casually stationing themselves at points of vantage on the deck—at the hatches, at the cabin door, along the taffrail. Mackay hurried to the captain. Thorn affected to ignore any danger, but he nevertheless ordered the anchors up. Seeing so many Indians still on board, the sailors hesitated. Thorn lost his head and uttered a shout. This served as a signal for the savages, who shrieked with derisive glee and fell upon the crew with knives, hatchets, and clubs. Down the companionway tumbled the ship's clerk, Lewis, stabbed in the back. Over the taffrail headlong fell Mackay, clubbed by the Indians aboard, caught on the knives of the squaws below. The captain was so unprepared for the attack that he had no weapon but his pocket-knife. He was stunned by a club, pitched overboard, and literally cut to pieces by the squaws. In a moment the *Tonquin* was a shambles. All on deck were slaughtered but four, who gained the main cabin, and with muskets aimed through windows scattered the yelling horde. The Indians sprang from the ship and drew off, while the four white survivors escaped in a boat, and the *Tonquin's* sails flapped idly in the wind. Next morning the Indians paddled out to plunder what seemed to be a deserted ship. A wounded white man appeared above the hatches and waved them to come on board and trade. They came in hosts, in hordes, in flocks, like carrion-birds or ants overrunning a half-dead thing. Suddenly earth and air at Clayoquot harbour were rent with a terrific explosion, and the sea was drenched with the blood of the slaughtered savages. The only remaining white man, the wounded Lewis, had blown up the powder magazine. He perished himself in order to punish the marauders.

—◊◊—

Had this story been known at Astoria when Thompson arrived, he would have found the Astorians in a thoroughly dejected condition. As it was, murmurs of discontent were heard. Here they had been marooned on the Columbia for three months without a ship, waiting for the contingent of the Astorians who were toiling across the continent.[2] Not thus did Nor'westers conduct expeditions. What

Thompson thought of the situation we do not know. All we do know is that he remained only a week. On July 22, fully provisioned by McDougall, he went back up the Columbia post-haste.

One year later we find Thompson at Fort William reporting the results of his expedition to the assembled directors of the North-West Company. He had surveyed every part of the Columbia from its source to its mouth. And he was the first white man on its upper waters.

The War of 1812 had begun, and a British warship was on its way to capture Astoria. At the same time the Nor'westers dispatched an overland expedition to the Columbia. Among their emissaries went the men of New Caledonia, Alexander Henry (the younger) of Rocky Mountain House, Donald McTavish, and a dozen others who were former comrades of the leading Astorians. They succeeded in their mission, and in the month of October 1813 Astor's fort was sold to the North-West Company and renamed Fort George.

The methods of fur traders have been the same the world over: to frighten a rival off the ground if possible; if not, then to buy him off. It is not all surmise to suppose that when Thompson was sent to the Pacific there was in view some other purpose than merely to survey an unknown river. But exploration and the fur trade went hand in hand; and whatever the motives may have been, the result was that, after more than four years of arduous toil, Thompson had given to commerce a great waterway. His exploration of the Columbia closes the period of discovery on the Pacific coast.

THE PASSING OF THE FUR LORDS

When Astoria passed to the Nor'westers, with it came, as we shall see, an opportunity of acquiring for Great Britain the whole of the vast region west of the Rockies, including California and Alaska. Gray's feat in finding the mouth of the Columbia, and the explorations of Lewis and Clark overland to the same river, gave the United States possession of a part of this territory by right of discovery; but this possession was practically superseded by the transfer of Astor's fort to the British-Canadian Company. Yet, to-day, we find Britain not in possession of California, not in possession of the region round the mouth of the Columbia, not in possession of Alaska. The reason for this will appear presently.

The Treaty of Ghent which closed the War of 1812 made no mention of the boundaries of Oregon, but it provided that any territory captured by either nation in the course of the war should be restored to the original owner. The question then arose: did this clause in the treaty apply to Astoria? Was the taking over of the fur-post by the British company in reality an act of war? The United States said Yes; Great Britain said No; and both nations claimed sovereignty over Oregon. In 1818 a provisional agreement was reached, under which either nation might trade and establish settlements in the disputed territory. But it was now utterly impossible for Astor to prosecute the fur trade on the Pacific. The 'Bostonnais' had lost prestige with the Indians when the *Tonquin* sank off Clayoquot, and the more experienced British and Canadian traders were in control of the field. At this time the Hudson's Bay Company and the Nor'westers were waging the trade war that terminated in their union in 1820–1821; and when the united companies came to assign officers to the different districts, John McLoughlin, who had been a partner in the North-West Company, was sent overland to rule Oregon.

What did Oregon comprise? At that time no man knew; but within ten years after his arrival in 1824 McLoughlin had sent out hunting brigades, consisting of two or three hundred horsemen, in all directions: east, under Alexander Ross, as far as Montana and Idaho; south, under Peter Skene Ogden, as far as Utah and Nevada and California; along the coast south as far as Monterey, under Tom Mackay, whose father had been murdered on the *Tonquin* and whose widowed mother had married McLoughlin; north, through New Caledonia, under James Douglas—'Black Douglas' they called the dignified, swarthy young Scotsman who later held supreme rule on the North Pacific as Sir James Douglas, the first governor of British Columbia. If one were to take a map of McLoughlin's transmontane empire and lay it across the face of a map of Europe, it would cover the continent from St. Petersburg to Madrid.

The ruler of this vast domain was one of the noblest men in the annals of the fur trade. John McLoughlin was a Canadian, born at Rivière du Loup, and he had studied medicine in Edinburgh. The Indians called him 'White Eagle,' from his long, snow-white hair and aquiline features. When McLoughlin reached Oregon—by canoe two thousand miles to the Rockies, by pack-horse and canoe another seven hundred miles south to the Columbia—two of the first things he saw were that Astoria, or Fort George, was too near the rum of trading schooners for the well-being of the Indians, and that it would be quite possible to raise food for his men on the spot, instead of transporting it over two watersheds and across the width of a continent. He at once moved the headquarters of the company from Astoria to a point on the north bank of the Columbia near the Willamette, where he erected Fort Vancouver. Then he sent his men overland to the Spaniards of Lower California to purchase seed-wheat and stock to begin farming in Oregon in order to provision the company's posts and brigades. It was about the time that his wheat-fields and orchards began to yield that some passing ocean traveller asked him: 'Do you think this country will ever be settled?' 'Sir,' answered McLoughlin, emphasizing his words by thumping his gold-headed cane on the floor, 'wherever wheat grows, men will go, and colonies will grow.' Afterwards, when he had to choose between loyalty to his company and saving the lives of thousands of American settlers who had come over the mountains destitute, these words of his were quoted against him. He had, according to the directors of the company, favoured settlement rather than the fur trade.

Meanwhile, McLoughlin ruled in a sort of rude baronial splendour on the banks of the Columbia. The 'Big House,' as the Indians always called the governor's mansion, stood in the centre of a spacious courtyard surrounded by palisades twenty feet high, with huge brass padlocks on the entrance-gates. Directly in front of the house two cannon were stationed, and piled up behind them ready for instant use were two pyramids of balls. Only officers of some rank dined in the Hall; and if visitors were present from coastal ships that ascended the river. Highland kilties stood behind the governor's chair playing the bagpipes. Towards autumn the southern and eastern brigades set out on their annual hunt in California, Nevada, Montana, and Idaho. Towards spring, when the upper rivers had cleared of ice, the northern brigades set out for the interior of New Caledonia. Nothing more picturesque was ever seen in the fur trade than these Oregon brigades. French-Canadian hunters with their Indian wives would be gathered to the number of two hundred. Indian ponies fattened during the summer on the deep pasturage of the Willamette or the plains of Walla Walla would be brought in to the fort and furbished forth in gayest of trappings. Provisions would then be packed on their backs. An eager crowd of wives and sweethearts and children would dash out for a last good-bye. The governor would personally shake hands with every departing hunter. Then to bugle-call the riders mounted their restive ponies, and the captain—Tom Mackay or Ogden or Ross—would lead the winding cavalcade into the defiles of mountain and forest, whence perhaps they would not emerge for a year and a half. Though the brigades numbered as many as two hundred men, they had to depend for food on the rifles of the hunters, except for flour and tobacco and bacon supplied at the fort. Once the brigade passed out of sight of the fort, the hunters usually dashed ahead to anticipate the stampeding of game by the long, noisy, slow-moving line. Next to the hunters would come the old bell-mare, her bell tinkling through the lonely silences. Far in the rear came the squaws and trappers. Going south, the aim was to reach the traverse of the deserts during winter, so that snow would be available for water. Going east, the aim was to cross the mountain passes before snow-fall. Going north, the canoes must ascend the upper rivers before ice formed. But times without number trappers and hunters were caught in the desert without snow for water; or were blocked in the mountain passes by blizzards; or were wrecked by the ice cutting their canoes on the upper rivers. Innumerable place-names commemorate the presence of humble trapper and hunter coursing the wilderness in the Oregon brigades. For example: Sublette's River, Payette's River, John Day's River, the Des Chutes, and many others. Indeed, many of the place-names commemorate the deaths of lonely hunters in the desert. Crow and Blackfoot and Sioux Indians often raided the brigades when on the home trip loaded with peltry. One can readily believe that rival traders from the Missouri instigated some of these raids. There were years when, of two hundred hunters setting out, only forty or fifty returned; there were years when the

John McLoughlin.
PHOTOGRAPHED BY SAVANNAH FROM AN ORIGINAL PAINTING

Hudson's Bay brigades found snow-bound, storm-bound, starving American hunters, and as a price for food exacted every peltry in the packs; and there were years when rival American traders bribed every man in Ogden's brigade to desert.

The New Caledonia brigades set out by canoe—huge, long, cedar-lined craft manned by fifty or even ninety men. These brigades were decked out gayest of all. Flags flew at the prow of each craft. Voyageurs adorned themselves with coloured sashes and headbands, with tinkling bells attached to the buckskin fringe of trouser-leg. Where the rivers narrowed to dark and shadowy canyons, the bag-pipes would skirl out some Highland air, or the French voyageurs would strike up some song of the habitant, paddling and chanting in perfect rhythm, and sometimes beating time with their paddles on the gunwales. Leaders of the canoe brigades understood well the art of never permitting fear to enter the souls of their voyageurs. Where the route might be exposed to Indian raid, a regale of rum would be dealt out; and the captain would keep the men paddling so hard there was no time for thought of danger.

In course of time the northern brigades no longer attempted to ascend the entire way to the interior of New Caledonia by boat. Boats and canoes would be left on the Columbia at Fort Colville or at Fort Okanagan (both south of the present international boundary), and the rest of the trail would be pursued by pack-horse. Kamloops became the great half-way house of these north-bound brigades; and horses were left there to pasture on the high, dry plains, while fresh horses were taken to ascend the mountain trails. Fort St. James on Stuart Lake became the chief post of New Caledonia. Here ruled young James Douglas, who had married the daughter of the chief factor William Connolly. Ordinarily, the fort on the blue alpine lake lay asleep like an August day; but on the occasion of a visit by the governor or the approach of a brigade, the drowsy post became a thing of life. Boom of cannon, firing of rifles, and skirling of bag-pipes welcomed the long cavalcade. The captain of the brigade as he entered the fort usually wore a high and pompous beaver hat, a velvet cloak lined with red silk, and knee-breeches with elaborate Spanish embossed-leather leggings. All this show was, of course, for the purpose of impressing the Indians. Whether impressed or not, the Indians always counted the days to the wild riot of feasting and boat-races and dog-races and horse-races that marked the arrival or departure of a brigade.

New Caledonia, as we know, is now a part of Canada; but why does not the Union Jack float over the great region beyond the Rockies to the south—south of the Strait of Juan de Fuca and the 49th parallel? Over all this territory British fur lords once held sway. California was in the limp fingers of Mexico, but the British traders were operating there, and had ample opportunity to secure it by purchase long before it passed to the United States in 1848. Sir George Simpson, the resident governor of the Hudson's Bay Company, advised the company to purchase it, but the directors in London could not see furs in the suggestion. Simpson would have gone further, and reached out the company's long arm to the islands of the Pacific and negotiated with the natives for permission to build a fort in Hawaii. James Douglas was for buying all Alaska from the Russians; but to the directors of the Hudson's Bay Company, Alaska seemed as remote and as worthless as Siberia, so they contented themselves with leasing a narrow strip along the shore. Thus California, Alaska, and Hawaii might easily have become British territory; but the opportunity was lost, and they went to the United States. So, too, did the fine territory of Oregon, out of which three states were afterwards added to the American Union. But the history of Oregon is confused in a maze of politics, into which we cannot enter here. As we have seen, Bruno Heceta, acting for Spain, was the first mariner to sight the Columbia, and the American, Robert Gray, was the first to enter its mouth, thus proving Heceta's conjecture of a great river. Then for Great Britain came Vancouver and Broughton; then the Americans, Lewis and Clark and the Astorians; and finally

Fort Vancouver.

Thompson, the British Nor'wester and the first man to explore the great river from its source to the sea. Then during the War of 1812 the American post on the Columbia passed to the North-West Company of Montreal; and if it had not been for the 'joint occupancy' agreement between Great Britain and the United States in 1818, Oregon would undoubtedly have remained British. But with the 'joint occupancy' arrangement leaving sovereignty in dispute, McLoughlin of Oregon knew well that in the end sovereignty would be established, as always, by settlement.

First came Jedediah Smith, the American fur trader, overland. He was robbed to the shirt on his back by Indians at the Umpqua river. There and then came the great choice to McLoughlin—should he save the life of rivals, or leave them to be murdered by Indians? He sent Tom Mackay to the Umpqua, punished the robber Indians, secured the pilfered furs, and paid the American for them. Then came American missionaries overland—the Lees and Whitman. Then came Wyeth, the trader and colonizer from Boston. The company fought Wyeth's trade and bought him out; but when the turbulent Indians crowded round the 'White Eagle,' chief of Fort Vancouver, asking, 'Shall we kill—shall we kill the "Bostonnais"?' McLoughlin struck the chief plotter down, drove the others from the fort, and had it noised about among the tribes that if any one struck the white 'Bostonnais,' McLoughlin would strike him. At the same time, McLoughlin earnestly desired that the territory should remain British. In 1838, at a council of the directors in London, he personally urged the sending of a garrison of British soldiers, and that the government should take control of Oregon in order to establish British rights. His suggestions received little consideration. Had not the company single-handed held all Rupert's Land for almost two hundred years? Had they not triumphed over all rivals? They would do so here.

But by 1843 immigrants were pouring over the mountains by the thousands. Washington Irving's *Astoria* and *Captain Bonneville*, and the political cry of 'Fifty-four forty or fight'—which meant American possession of all south of Alaska—had roused the attention of the people of the United States to the merits of Oregon, and caused them to make extravagant claims. Long before the Oregon Treaty of 1846, which established the 49th parallel as the boundary, McLoughlin had foreseen what was coming. The movement from the east had become a tide. The immigrants who came over the Oregon Trail in 1843 were starving, almost naked, and without a roof. Again the Indians crowded about McLoughlin. 'Shall we kill? Shall we kill?' they asked. McLoughlin took the rough American overlanders into his fort, fed them, advanced them provisions on credit, and sent them to settle on the Willamette. Some of them showed their ingratitude later by denouncing McLoughlin as 'an aristocrat and a tyrant.' The settlers established a provisional government in 1844, and joined in the rallying-cry of 'Fifty-four forty or fight.' This, as McLoughlin well knew, was the beginning of the end. His friends among the colonists begged him to subscribe to the provisional government in order that they might protect his fort from some of their number who threatened to 'burn it about his ears.' He had appealed to the British government for protection, but no answer had come; and at length, after a hard struggle and many misgivings, he cast in his lot with the Americans. Two years later, in 1846, he retired from the service of the company and went to live among the settlers. He died at Oregon City on the Willamette in 1857.

—⁂—

As early as June 1842 McLoughlin had sent Douglas prospecting in Vancouver Island, which was north of the immediate zone of dispute, for a site on which to erect a new post. The Indian village of Camosun, the Cordoba of the old Spanish charts, stood on the site of the present city of Victoria. Here was fresh water; here was a good harbour; here was shelter from outside gales. Across the sea lay islands ever green in a climate always mild and salubrious. Fifteen men left old Fort Vancouver with Douglas in March 1843 in the company's ship the *Beaver*, and anchored at Vancouver Island, just outside Camosun Bay. With Douglas went the Jesuit missionary, Father Bolduc, who on March 19 celebrated the first Mass ever said on Vancouver Island, and afterwards baptized Indians till he was fairly exhausted. In three days Douglas had a well dug and timbers squared. For every forty pickets erected by the Indians he gave them a blanket. By September stockades and houses had been completed, and as many as fifty men had come to live at the new fort, to which the name Victoria was finally given. Victoria became the headquarters of the Hudson's Bay Company on the Pacific. It was unique as a fortified post, in that it was built without the driving of a single nail, wooden pegs being used instead.

By 1849 the discovery of gold in California was bringing a rush of overlanders. There had been rumours of the discovery of precious metals on the Fraser and in East Kootenay. The company became alarmed; and Sir John Pelly, the governor in England, and Sir George

The Fort of the Hudson's Bay Company, Victoria, BC.
FROM A PHOTOGRAPH BY SAVANNAH

Simpson, the governor in America, went to the British government with the disquieting question: What is to hinder American colonists rolling north of the boundary and establishing right of possession there as they did on the Columbia? By no stretch of its charter could the Hudson's Bay Company claim feudal rights west of the Rockies. What, my Lord Grey asks, would the company advise the British government to do to avert this danger from a tide of democracy rolling north? Why, of course, answers Sir John Pelly, proclaim Vancouver Island a British colony and give the company a grant of the territory and the company will colonize it with British subjects. The proposal was laid before parliament. It would be of no profit to follow the debate that ensued in the House of Commons, which was chiefly 'words without knowledge darkening counsel.' The request was officially granted in January 1849; and Richard Blanshard, a barrister of London, was dispatched as governor of the new colony. But as he had neither salary nor subjects, he went back to England in disgust in 1851, and James Douglas of the Hudson's Bay Company reigned in his stead.

But fate again played the unexpected part, and rang down the curtain on the fur lords of the Pacific coast. A few years previously Douglas had seen McLoughlin compelled to choose between loyalty to his company and loyalty to humanity. A choice between his country and his company was now unexpectedly thrust on the reticent, careful, masterful Douglas. In 1856 gold was discovered in the form of large nuggets on the Fraser and the Thompson, and adventurers poured into the country—20,000 in a single year. Douglas foresaw that this meant British empire on the Pacific and that the supremacy of the fur traders was about to pass away. The British government bought back Vancouver Island, and proclaimed the new colony of British Columbia on the mainland. Douglas retired from the company's service and was appointed governor of both colonies.

In 1866 they were united under one government. The stampede of treasure-seekers up the Fraser is another story. When the new colony on the mainland came into being, and the Hudson's Bay Company fell from the rank of a feudal overlord to that of a private trader, the pioneer days of the Pacific became a thing of the past.

ENDNOTES

'Alexander Mackenzie, From Canada, By Land'

[1] See another volume of this Series, *Adventures of the Far North*, chap. iii.

[2] The Takulli, This tribe cremated the dead, and the widows collected the ashes of their dead husbands and carried them during a period of three years: hence the name 'Carriers.'

Thompson and the Astorians

[1] To explain what may appear like a confusion of names, it may be stated that in the history of the fur trade from 1800 to 1850 there were at various stages as many as sixteen differently situated fur-posts under the name of Rocky Mountain House.

[2] The overland party suffered the greatest hardship and some loss of life, and did not arrive at Astoria till January 1812.

BIBLIOGRAPHICAL NOTE

The bibliography of the Pacific is enormous. There is, indeed, a record of discovery and exploration on the Pacific coast almost as large as that of New France or New England. Only a few of the principal books can be mentioned here; but in most of these will be found good bibliographies which will point the reader to original sources, if he wishes to pursue the subject.

ON DRAKE. *Drake and the Tudor Navy*, in two volumes, by Julian Corbett (1898); *Sir Francis Drake*, by the same author (1890), in the 'English Men of Action' series; *The World Encompassed*, by Francis Fletcher (1628). See also the article on Drake in the *Dictionary of National Biography*.

ON VITUS BERING AND THE RUSSIANS. *Peter the Great*, by Williams (1859); *Peter the Great*, by Motley (1877); Coxe's *Discoveries of the Russians* (1781); Lauridsen's *Vitus Bering* (1885); Laut's *Vikings of the Pacific* (1905).

ON COOK AND VANCOUVER. Cook's *Voyage to the Pacific Ocean* (1784); Ledyard's *Journal of Cook's Last Voyage* (1783); Sir Walter Besant's *Captain Cook* (1890), in the 'English Men of Action' series; Kitson's *Captain James Cook, the Circumnavigator* (1907); Vancouver's *Voyage of Discovery to the North Pacific Ocean* (1798). See also the articles on Cook and Vancouver in the *Dictionary of National Biography*.

ON THE EXPLORATIONS OF MACKENZIE, FRASER, AND THOMPSON. Mackenzie's *Voyages* (1801); Burpee's *Search for the Western Sea* (1908); *Fur Traders of the Far West* by Alexander Ross (1855); Laut's *Conquest of the Great Northwest* (1908); *Canada and its Provinces*, vol. iv (1914).

ON THE FUR TRADERS BEYOND THE ROCKIES. Morice's *History of the Northern Interior of British Columbia* (1904); *Sir James Douglas*, by Coats and Gosnell (1908), in the 'Makers of Canada' series; *Canada and its Provinces*, vol. xxi (1914); Bancroft's *History of the Northwest Coast* (1884), and his *History of Oregon* (1888); Lyman's *History of Oregon* (1903). For an exhaustive statement of the Oregon Boundary Question, see the article, 'Boundary Disputes and Treaties,' by James White, in *Canada and its Provinces*, vol. viii.

INDEX

THE CLASSICS WEST COLLECTION
Capturing the spirit of the Canadian West

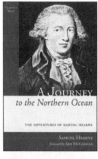  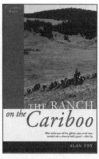 

 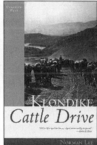 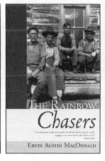 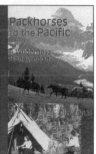

A Journey to the Northern Ocean
The Adventures of Samuel Hearne
Samuel Hearne
978-1-894898-60-7 · 5.5 x 8.5 · 336 pages · $19.95 pb

Three Against the Wilderness
Eric Collier
978-1-894898-54-6 · 5.5 x 8.5 · 288 pages · $19.95 pb

The Ranch on the Cariboo
Alan Fry
978-1-926741-00-0 · 5.5 x 8.5 · 288 pages · $19.95 pb

Cheadle's Journal
Of Trip Across Canada, 1862–1863
Walter B. Cheadle
978-1-926741-07-9 · 5.5 x 8.5 · 312 pages · $19.95 pb

Harmon's Journal 1800–1819
Daniel Williams Harmon
978-1-894898-44-7 · 5.5 x 8.5 · 288 pages · $19.95 pb

Klondike Cattle Drive
Norman Lee
978-1-894898-14-0 · 5.5 x 8.5 · 96 pages · $12.95 pb

The Rainbow Chasers
Ervin Austin MacDonald
978-1-894898-30-0 · 5.5 x 8.5 · 296 pages · $19.95 pb

Packhorses to the Pacific
A Wilderness Honeymoon
Cliff Kopas
978-1894898-13-3 · 5.5 x 8.5 · 192 pages · $17.95 pb

AGNES C. LAUT was born in Huron County, Ontario in 1871. She was raised and educated in Winnipeg, and worked briefly as a teacher prior to a bout of tuberculosis that changed the course of her life. She became a reporter and editorial writer for the *Manitoba Free Press* in the 1890s, then a wide-ranging travel writer. Her books include *Lords of the North*, *Heralds of Empire*, *The Story of the Trapper*, *Pathfinders of the West*, *Vikings of the Pacific*, *Canada at the Crossroads*, and *The Romance of the Rails*. She died in 1936.